Praise for *Collective Efficacy* by Jenni Donohoo

We knew that collective efficacy mattered, but Donohoo, in this easy-to-read, research-based book, makes it abundantly clear that schools need to focus on working together and believing in each other's ability to make a difference. Donohoo combines a synthesis of the research around collective efficacy with practical strategies and tools for how to create the right conditions for this skill set to flourish in schools.

**—Jennifer Abrams, Educational Consultant and Author
of *Having Hard Conversations, Hard Conversations
Unpacked,* and *The Multi-Generational Workplace*
Palo Alto, CA**

In *Collaborative Inquiry for Educators: A Facilitator's Guide to School Improvement* (2013), Donohoo described what collaborative inquiry is and how to do it. In *The Transformative Power of Collaborative Inquiry: Realizing Change in Schools and Classrooms* (2016), Donohoo and Velasco explained how collaborative inquiry can bring change to individuals and systems. Now in her new book, *Collective Efficacy: How Educators' Beliefs Impact Student Learning,* Donohoo shares the personal impact collaborative inquiry can have on teaching collectively and individually.

In a time when educators are under increased scrutiny and criticism, Donohoo builds a case using research and experiences as the foundation of how collaborative inquiry can improve the disposition and practice of teachers. Sprinkled with thought-provoking questions throughout the book, Donohoo encourages teachers and leaders to reflect on their practice to determine their own path to build a personal philosophy and collective belief set that all children can succeed.

**—Martin Chaffee, Leadership Consultant for School
Administrators, Oakland Schools, Waterford, MI**

Collective efficacy beliefs can be inferred from the conversations we have in schools. If we do not provoke such conversations, question assumptions, and consider new possibilities, we remain in a stuck state. Donohoo's work is both timely and important. It interrogates the concept of collective teacher efficacy, providing a clarity and understanding that feeds into a framework that will change those conversations, ensuring school movement and a culture of shared and high expectations.

**—Simon Feasey, Head Teacher (School Principal),
Bader Primary School, Thornaby-on-Tees, Stockton, UK**

Acclaimed staff developer and experienced educational consultant Jenni Donohoo puts the sword to the mistaken idea that the best way to improve teaching is by evaluating individuals. Donohoo takes an old idea—collective efficacy—strengthens it with a rigorous research base, and brings it alive through her countless observations of teachers' practice.

Collective Efficacy is about the overwhelming power that teachers have to improve student learning and achievement when they work together, explore every avenue open to them, and persist relentlessly once they have found the best ways forward. This book will turn many people's assumptions about how best to improve student achievement on their head. Probably one of the very best education books of the year.

—Andy Hargreaves, Brennan Chair in Education, Boston College, Chestnut Hill, MA

Jenni Donohoo has written a timely, compelling, and wonderfully practical book that will help leaders develop a stronger sense of collective efficacy in their schools. As Donohoo points out so clearly, what "we" as a collective believe we can achieve together makes a significant difference. Our beliefs impact our actions which, in turn, impact our collective sense of competence, confidence, and responsibility as professionals. Our actions can also change our beliefs through the work we do together. *Collective Efficacy* offers many strategies, including the use of protocols for leaders that can be used to nurture school cultures where collective efficacy through impactful collaboration can take root, grow, and thrive. While what we do as individual educators in our classrooms will always be important, what we can accomplish as a collaborative collective of professionals can change learning and growth trajectories for a whole school community.

—Beate Planche, EdD, Educational Consultant, Collaborative Learning Services, Coach, and Co-Author of *Leading Collaborative Learning: Empowering Excellence* Newmarket, ON

A powerful guide for leaders wanting to unleash the impact of teachers! Donohoo masterfully bridges the theory–practice divide, providing compelling evidence of why and how educators' beliefs impact student learning and the results when teachers build their collective efficacy. The blend of practical strategies and a compelling four-stage collaborative leadership inquiry model make this a must read for every education leader.

—Joanne Quinn, Co-Author of *Coherence: The Right Drivers in Action for Schools, Districts, and Systems*, and Consultant, Michael Fullan Enterprises and New Pedagogies for Deep Learning, Toronto, ON

Collective efficacy has been a rather elusive topic ever since Professor John Hattie indicated that this subject would top his list of 150 influences in his Visible Learning research. Dr. Jenni Donohoo has seized the opportunity to take this work deeper and has, for me at least, provided the first really clear and comprehensive analysis of what efficacy is all about.

This book is a thorough examination of the subject of efficacy in all its forms dating back to the work of Albert Bandura, who really first made mention of this notion. Dr. Donohoo has worked hard to uncover the extensive research base for the subject of efficacy and makes a sound case for the impact of collective efficacy in schools and organizations.

Dr. Donohoo's previous work on collaborative inquiry is enhanced by this, her most recent examination of the collaborative process, which is her current passion and the focus of much of her writing and presenting.

What adds great value apart from the extensive research base to support this notion of efficacy is the manner in which she makes this work come alive with suggestions for practical application. While there is lots of theoretical background, Dr. Donohoo has taken time to make it applicable and practical for collaborative teams with robust resources filled with useful protocols teams can apply immediately.

This is a very helpful and valuable resource for any school leader and any group who see themselves working in a collaborative, team environment.

—Ainsley B. Rose, President, Thistle Educational Development Inc., and Corwin Author Consultant West Kelowna, BC

Collective Efficacy

Collective Efficacy

How Educators' Beliefs Impact Student Learning

Jenni Donohoo

A JOINT PUBLICATION

FOR INFORMATION:

Corwin

A SAGE Company

2455 Teller Road

Thousand Oaks, California 91320

(800) 233-9936

www.corwin.com

SAGE Publications Ltd.

1 Oliver's Yard

55 City Road

London EC1Y 1SP

United Kingdom

SAGE Publications India Pvt. Ltd.

B 1/I 1 Mohan Cooperative Industrial Area

Mathura Road, New Delhi 110 044

India

SAGE Publications Asia-Pacific Pte. Ltd.

3 Church Street

#10-04 Samsung Hub

Singapore 049483

Program Director: Dan Alpert

Senior Associate Editor: Kimberly Greenberg

Editorial Assistant: Katie Crilley

Production Editor: Melanie Birdsall

Copy Editor: Deanna Noga

Typesetter: C&M Digitals (P) Ltd.

Proofreader: Lawrence W. Baker

Indexer: Molly Hall

Cover Designer: Michael Dubowe

Marketing Manager: Charline Maher

Printed in the United States of America

Library of Congress Cataloging-in-Publication Data

Names: Donohoo, Jenni, author.

Title: Collective efficacy : how educators' beliefs impact student learning / Jenni Donohoo.

Description: Thousand Oaks, California : Corwin, 2016. | Includes bibliographical references and index.

Identifiers: LCCN 2016030574 | ISBN 9781506356495 (pbk. : alk. paper)

Subjects: LCSH: Teacher effectiveness. | School improvement programs.

Classification: LCC LB1025.3 .D67 2016 | DDC 371.102—dc23

LC record available at https://lccn.loc.gov/2016030574

This book is printed on acid-free paper.

MIX
Paper from
responsible sources
FSC® C012947
www.fsc.org

17 18 19 20 10 9 8 7 6 5 4 3

Contents

List of Figures and Tables

FIGURES

TABLES

Preface

Fostering collective teacher efficacy is a timely and important issue if we are going to realize success for all students. When a school staff shares the belief that through their collective actions they can positively influence student outcomes, student achievement increases. Collective teacher efficacy deserves the attention of every educator because it was recently ranked as the *number one factor* influencing student achievement (Hattie, 2016). Educators with high efficacy show greater effort and persistence, a willingness to try new teaching approaches, and attend more closely to the needs of students who are not progressing well. They also convey high expectations, foster learner autonomy, and welcome increased parental involvement. In addition, educators who share a sense of collective efficacy get students to believe they can excel in school.

Efficacy beliefs are very powerful because they guide educators' actions and behavior. Efficacy beliefs help determine what educators focus on, how they respond to challenges, and how they expend their efforts. When staffs lack a sense of collective efficacy, they do not pursue certain courses of action because they feel they lack the capabilities to achieve positive outcomes. If educators' realities are filtered through the belief that they can do *very little* to influence student achievement, then it is very likely these beliefs will be manifested in their practice. It is promising to know that educators' beliefs about their capability to impact student outcomes can be shaped and adjusted.

Research in this field is emerging, and more is becoming known about the factors that influence the collective efficacy of a school staff. The purpose of this book is two-fold: (a) to translate the extant research on collective teacher efficacy into a form that is useable by principals and teachers; and (b) to provide practical strategies, tools, and an inquiry framework to help bridge the theory-practice divide. In this book, readers will find

- A rationale for strengthening collective teacher efficacy
- Sources that influence collective teacher efficacy
- A list of enabling conditions for collective teacher efficacy to flourish

- Successful leadership practices that hold the potential to strengthen efficacy
- Efficacy enhancing professional learning structures and protocols
- A framework to organize leadership actions for strengthening the collective efficacy of a school staff

Strengthening collective teacher efficacy as a change strategy in schools is a very different approach to bringing about change than what has been done in the past. It is not *another initiative*, usually resulting in teachers rolling their eyes when introduced. It does not require the purchase of expensive programs or new resources. It does not require costly retraining. It does, however, require determination and stamina on the part of leaders and leadership teams. It requires that awareness be built about collective efficacy and its importance in relation to student achievement. It requires that structures and processes be put in place for teachers to come together to solve problems of practice collaboratively. It requires that leaders resist the temptation to direct action and rather empower teachers by involving them in meaningful issues related to school improvement. It also requires that teams of teachers are supported and feedback is provided when interpreting the result of their collective actions.

Understanding what it is, why it is important, and the positive consequences associated with it is the first step. If efficacy beliefs are going to be reshaped, then gaining insight into how collective efficacy beliefs are formed is important as well. Examining school characteristics associated with improved collective teacher efficacy will help readers in determining potential transferable aspects of successful change strategies. Knowing how and why certain professional learning structures and protocols help foster collective efficacy will help educators and facilitators in selecting and utilizing them to their fullest. Finally, by engaging in an inquiry approach to examine ways to strengthen the efficacy of a staff, formal and informal leaders will determine what works and adjust approaches to realize increased collective efficacy.

A key to turning around schools that struggle to support student learning lies in the ability of formal and informal leaders to cultivate collective efficacy. Exemplary leadership practices highlighted in the research and considered highly effective in relation to developing collective teacher efficacy are presented throughout this book. Strategies for creating an organization of shared inquiry and decision making using student achievement data are outlined along with ways to create opportunities for meaningful collaboration and to empower teachers. In addition to the research, readers will find an inquiry framework and tools that will assist them in measuring the collective efficacy beliefs of the staff, determining the degree to which the enabling conditions are in place within their schools, implementing changes in leadership practice, monitoring results, and determining next steps.

Acknowledgments

I would like to thank my family and friends for their patience with me while I wrote this book. I would especially like to thank my editor, Dan Alpert, for his enthusiasm for this book, support in making it happen, and valuable feedback throughout the writing process. I would like to acknowledge the following amazing people in the Corwin family: Mike Soules, Lisa Shaw, Kristin Anderson, Kimberly Greenberg, Katie Crilley, Melanie Birdsall, and Charline Maher. I feel so fortunate to be part of the Corwin team.

I have benefited greatly from collaborating with educators in school districts, the provincial literacy leads and education officers in the Curriculum and Assessment Policy Branch at the Ontario Ministry of Education, Corwin authors and consultants, and friends from Learning Forward and the Ontario Institute for Studies in Education. I look forward to engaging in many more enriching conversations about issues related to improving student outcomes.

Finally, I'd like to acknowledge my husband, Jim Donohoo. This book was made possible because of Jim's encouragement, selflessness, and support.

About the Author

 **Jenni Donohoo** has been seconded to the Curriculum and Assessment Policy Branch in the Ontario Ministry of Education for the past few years. In this role, she works with system and school leaders to support high quality professional learning and improve adolescent literacy. Jenni earned a doctorate in education from the Joint Program at the University of Windsor, Brock and Lakehead in 2010. Since then, her passion for research and writing has grown. This is Jenni's third book with Corwin. Jenni lives with her husband and their two golden retrievers in a heritage home in historic Amherstburg, Ontario.

1 Collective Teacher Efficacy

Among the types of thoughts that affect action, none is more central or pervasive than people's judgments of their capabilities to deal effectively with different realities. (Bandura, 1986, p. 21)

Amazing things happen when a school staff shares the belief that they are able to achieve collective goals and overcome challenges to impact student achievement. Ranking as the greatest factor impacting student achievement (Hattie, 2016), collective teacher efficacy deserves the attention of every educator, everywhere. Collective teacher efficacy refers to the "collective self-perception that teachers in a given school make an educational difference to their students over and above the educational impact of their homes and communities" (Tschannen-Moran & Barr, 2004, p. 190). When teachers share that belief, it outranks *every other factor* in regard to impacting student achievement including socioeconomic status, prior achievement, home environment, and parental involvement.

Fostering collective teacher efficacy should be at the forefront of a planned strategic effort in all schools and school districts. Educators' beliefs about their ability to reach *all* students, including those who are unmotivated or disengaged, should be openly shared, discussed, and collectively developed. Given its effect on student achievement, strengthening collective teacher efficacy should be a top priority relevant to everyone in the field of education. Regardless of the subject area you teach, whether you belong to a staff in a large school or small school, a school located in an urban or a rural area, whether your students qualify for free and reduced lunch or come from affluent neighborhoods, have Individual Education Plans (IEPs) or are English language learners (ELLs), or whether

● 1

you are a formal or informal leader, it is important to consider how collective teacher efficacy beliefs come to fruition through the practices of educators. It is also important to understand the negative effects that occur when staffs do not share a sense of collective efficacy.

In this first chapter, readers are introduced to the concept of collective teacher efficacy and the effect size research that demonstrates the strong link between collective teacher efficacy and student achievement. Readers are introduced to sources that shape collective efficacy beliefs.

It is important to consider how collective teacher efficacy beliefs come to fruition through the practices of educators. It is also important to understand the negative effects that occur when staffs do not share a sense of collective efficacy.

WHAT IS COLLECTIVE TEACHER EFFICACY?

I recently met with school improvement teams at two secondary schools. Both schools' results on the Ontario Secondary School Literacy Test (OSSLT) were below the provincial average. The conversation at the first school was driven by the teachers sitting around the table. It centered on research, school-wide strategies, lessons learned from past experiences, and progress monitoring. Teachers' voices were heard because they were instrumental in determining next steps, which included designing professional learning for their peers.

Although the conversation at the second site was also driven by teachers, it was remarkably different. The teachers expressed concerns about burnout and the majority of the conversation was centered on the high-needs population they were trying to serve. The school had a high percentage of students with IEPs and ELLs. In addition, the majority of students came from low socioeconomic backgrounds. Unlike the staff at the first school who identified steps they could take to improve student learning, the staff at the second school felt there was nothing left to try, indicating "there is nothing that we can do to make a difference with these kids."

The staff at the first school faced similar demographic challenges but did not let that deter them. They believed that through their collaborative efforts, they could help students achieve—in measurable ways. This team demonstrated a strong sense of collective efficacy. The school improvement team at the second site believed that their efforts were in vain. Their belief was that student achievement could not be advanced—no matter what they did and regardless of whether they worked together or alone. There was no collective efficacy among this staff.

When teachers believe that together they and their colleagues can impact student achievement, they share a sense of collective teacher efficacy. Collective teacher efficacy refers to "the judgments of teachers in a school that the faculty as a whole can organize and execute the courses of action required to have a positive effect on students" (Goddard, Hoy, & Woolfolk Hoy, 2004, p. 4). Collective efficacy is high when teachers believe that the staff is capable of helping students master complex content, fostering students' creativity, and getting students to believe they can do well in school.

To better understand collective teacher efficacy, it is useful to consider the concept of *self-efficacy*, introduced almost 40 years ago by Bandura (1977). Bandura (1977) described a self-efficacy expectation as "the conviction that one can successfully execute the behavior required to produce outcomes" (p. 193). It is the belief, on the part of an individual, that he or she can perform the necessary activities to attain a desired outcome. Self-efficacy expectations are context specific. For example, a person might believe that he or she is capable of achieving a certain amount of weight loss. That efficacy expectation might shift during a time when the individual is staying at an all-inclusive resort.

Teacher self-efficacy refers to a teacher's belief that he or she can perform the necessary activities to influence student learning. Protheroe (2008) noted that the term *teacher efficacy* references "a teacher's sense of competence—not some objective measure of actual competence" (p. 43). These beliefs are also context specific and are formed as teachers weigh their perceptions of personal competence based on the task demands for a given situation (Goddard, 2001). For example, a teacher might feel that she is capable of increasing students' ability to master procedures and concepts in mathematics but is not as capable when it comes to teaching students how to develop a well-structured argument in an English class.

In the past decade, a more recent construct, *collective efficacy*, has received attention from researchers. Similar to an individual's belief in his or her competence, collective efficacy deals with a group's beliefs in its competence for successful outcomes. Researchers, for example, have examined the consequences of collective efficacy on responses to neighborhood problems (Browning, Burrington, Leventhal, & Brooks-Gunn, 2008; Wells, Schafer, Varano, & Bynum, 2006), and how collective efficacy affects political interests (Reichert, 2015) and environmental behavior (Bonniface & Henley, 2008).

As noted earlier, *collective teacher efficacy* refers to teachers in a school characterized by an attitude that together they can make a difference for students. It too is context specific because beliefs are formed based on an analysis of teachers' perceptions about the teaching competence of the school staff, the difficulties inherent in the educational task facing the school, as well as the supports available in the setting (Goddard, 2001). Goddard, Hoy, and Woolfolk Hoy (2000) noted that "analogous to self-efficacy, collective teacher efficacy is associated with the tasks, level of effort, persistence, shared thoughts, stress levels, and achievement of groups" (p. 482).

The concept of *collective teacher efficacy* has also received increased attention from educational researchers since the time Bandura (1993) demonstrated that the effect of perceived collective efficacy on student achievement was stronger than the link between socioeconomic status and student achievement. Consistent findings have been reported in a number of studies since. For example, Ramos, Silva, Pontes, Fernandez, and Nina (2014) conducted a systematic review of research published between 2000 and 2013 on collective teacher efficacy. Thirty-nine percent of the articles reviewed investigated the relationship between collective teacher efficacy and student performance. In every one of these studies a positive correlation between the two constructs was found. Ramos et al. (2014) also noted that when collective efficacy beliefs were elevated, the negative effects of sociodemographic aspects were reduced. Goddard et al. (2000) found that collective teacher efficacy was a more significant predictor of student achievement than socioeconomic status in both mathematics and reading in elementary schools. In a study examining mathematics achievement in high schools, Hoy, Sweetland, and Smith (2002) found that collective efficacy "was more important in explaining school achievement than socio-economic status" (p. 89). Moolenaar, Sleegers, and Daly (2012) found that "perceived collective efficacy was positively associated with increased language achievement, above the influence of socioeconomic status" (p. 257) in elementary schools.

WHY IS COLLECTIVE TEACHER EFFICACY IMPORTANT?

In addition to socioeconomic status, there are hundreds of other factors that influence student achievement. How does collective teacher efficacy compare to other factors? Like socioeconomic status, some of these contributions come from the home, such as parental involvement and home environment. Some include contributions from the students themselves, such as students' estimates of their own performance (also known as *students' expectations*), prior achievement, and motivation. Other factors that influence achievement come from teachers and teaching approaches. A few examples include teacher–student relationships, teacher clarity, feedback, homework, and prompting for metacognition. Finally, other factors influencing achievement include contributions from the school and the curriculum, such as collective teacher efficacy, school size, school leadership, and/or school programs including play, phonics, and mathematics programs to name a few. With so many possible influences, the following questions come to mind:

1. Which influences have the *greatest impact* on student achievement?

2. How strong is the link between collective teacher efficacy and student achievement?

At the beginning of his career, John Hattie set out to determine the answer to the first question and in 2009 published *Visible Learning: A Synthesis of Over 800 Meta-Analyses Relating to Achievement*. Hattie continues to update his synthesis, which now includes an additional 400 studies. Recently, Hattie ranked collective teacher efficacy as the number *one*

> An effect size emphasizes the difference in magnitude of given approaches for purposes of comparison. An effect size of 0 reveals that the influence had no effect on student achievement. The larger the effect size, the more powerful the influence. Hattie (2009) suggested an effect size of 0.2 is relatively small, an effect size of 0.4 is medium, and an effect size of 0.6 is large. Readers should keep this in mind as they consider the effect sizes for the various influences reported throughout this book.

factor influencing student achievement (Hattie, 2016) based on a meta-analysis by Eells (2011). Eells's (2011) meta-analysis demonstrated that collective efficacy and student achievement were strongly related with an effect size of 1.57. According to the Visible Learning Research (Hattie, 2012), this is more than double the effect size of feedback.

Table 1.1 displays some of the factors that influence student achievement and their effect sizes. With an effect size of 0.52, socioeconomic status is a powerful influence, as compared to school leadership (0.39) or homework (0.29), for example. Collective teacher efficacy, however, is beyond three times more powerful and predictive than socioeconomic status. It is also greater than three times more likely to influence student achievement than student motivation and concentration, persistence, and engagement.

Collective teacher efficacy, as an influence on student achievement, is a contribution that comes from the school—not the home and not the students themselves. It is more than double the effect of prior achievement and more than triple the effect of home environment and parental involvement. This supports Marzano's (2003) conclusion, based on his analysis of

Table 1.1 Factors Influencing Student Achievement and Their Effect Size

INFLUENCE	EFFECT SIZE
Collective teacher efficacy	1.57
Self-reported grades/student expectations	1.44
Teacher clarity	0.75
Feedback	0.75
Teacher-student relationships	0.72
Metacognitive strategies	0.69
Prior achievement	0.65
Phonics instruction	0.54
Socioeconomic status	0.52
Home environment	0.52
Play programs	0.50
Parental involvement	0.49
Motivation	0.48
Concentration/persistence/engagement	0.48
School size	0.43
Mathematics programs	0.40
School leadership	0.39
Homework	0.29

Source: Adapted from Hattie, J. (2012). *Visible learning for teachers: Maximizing impact on learning.* New York, NY: Routledge; and Hattie, J. (2016, July). *Mindframes and Maximizers.* 3rd Annual Visible Learning Conference held in Washington, DC.

research conducted over thirty-five years, that "schools that are highly effective produce results that almost entirely overcome the effects of student backgrounds" (p. 7). Research shows that at the school level, collective teacher efficacy beliefs contribute significantly to the school's level of academic success.

Bandura (1977) noted that "the strength of people's convictions in their own effectiveness is likely to affect whether they will even try to cope with given situations" (p. 193). Efficacy beliefs are very powerful as they guide our actions and behavior. Efficacy beliefs help to determine our focus, response to challenges, and effort expenditure. "Perceptions of collective efficacy directly affect the diligence and resolve with which groups choose to pursue their goals" (Goddard et al., 2004, p. 8). If educators' realities are filtered through the belief that they can do very little to influence student achievement, then it is very likely these beliefs will be manifested in their practice. If, however, teachers share a sense of collective efficacy, research demonstrates it is the greatest factor that impacts student achievement (Hattie, 2016).

> *If educators' realities are filtered through the belief that they can do very little to influence student achievement, then it is very likely these beliefs will be manifested in their practice.*

To foster collective teacher efficacy as part of a planned strategic effort for improving student achievement, it is important to understand how collective efficacy beliefs are formed. Collective teacher efficacy is malleable and shaped through the cognitive processing and interpretation of events based on causal attributions and the group's assessment of the task and competency of the team. These ideas along with four sources of collective efficacy are addressed in the section that follows.

> "A theory that denies that thoughts can regulate actions does not lend itself readily to the explanation of complex human behavior." (Bandura, 1986, p. 15)

EFFICACY SHAPING INFORMATION

It is promising to know that beliefs about our capabilities to impact student outcomes can be adjusted. How exactly are efficacy beliefs influenced? There are four sources that shape an individual's efficacy beliefs. Causal attributions also significantly contribute to collective sense of efficacy (Bandura, 1993). Along with causal attributions and the four sources of efficacy information, collective sense of efficacy is shaped through task analysis, including factors that constitute or inhibit success, the context, materials, and resources required for success (Goddard et al., 2004).

> "People process, weigh, and integrate diverse sources of information concerning their capability, and they regulate their choice of behavior and effort expenditure accordingly." (Bandura, 1977, p. 212)

Four Sources of Efficacy

Four sources shaping collective efficacy beliefs include mastery experiences, vicarious experiences, social persuasion, and affective states (Bandura, 1986; Goddard et al., 2004). The most powerful source of collective teacher efficacy is mastery experiences. Basically, when teams experience success (mastery) and attribute that success to causes within their control, collective efficacy increases and teams come to expect that effective performances can be repeated. Goddard et al. (2004) explained that teachers experience successes and failures and "past school successes build teachers' beliefs in the capability of the faculty, whereas failures tend to undermine a sense of collective efficacy" (p. 5). Past levels of school success help influence a staff's belief in their capability to make a difference for students.

"After strong efficacy expectations are developed through repeated success, the negative impact of occasional failures is likely to be reduced." (Bandura, 1977, p. 195)

The second most powerful source of collective efficacy is vicarious experiences. When school staffs see others who are faced with similar opportunities and challenges perform well, expectations are generated that they too can overcome obstacles. Collective teacher efficacy is enhanced when teams of educators observe success in school environments similar to their own. Vicarious experiences can occur through site visits, watching video, networking, or reading about it.

The third source, social persuasion, has the potential to influence collective efficacy when groups are encouraged by credible and trustworthy persuaders to innovate and overcome challenges. The more believable the source of the information, the more likely are efficacy expectations to change (Bandura, 1977). Adams and Forsyth (2006) noted that social persuasion "depends on establishing norms of openness, collaboration, and cooperation" (p. 631). Social persuasion at the collective level consists of members of the school staff persuading other teachers that they constitute an effective team. Goddard et al. (2000) noted that the more cohesive the faculty, the more likely they are to be persuaded by sound arguments.

The fourth and least influential source, affective states, includes feelings of excitement or anxiety associated with an individual's perceptions of his or her capability or incompetence. Goddard et al. (2004) noted that although there is little research on the impact of affective states on organizations, "affective states may influence how organizations interpret and react to the myriad challenges they face" (p. 6). Tschannen-Moran and Barr (2004) refer to this as "the emotional tone of the organization" (p. 190).

Finally, Bandura (1977) noted that "people rely partly on their state of physiological arousal in judging their anxiety and vulnerability to stress" (p. 198).

> Easton High School is faced with the challenge that 4 years in a row reading comprehension scores on the state test remain stagnant and below the state standard. The school is located in an urban area with high poverty rates and single parent households. The school improvement team is tasked with the challenge to create a plan to increase reading comprehension scores over the next 2 years. There is no collective efficacy among the Easton High School staff. Below are excerpts from the dialogue that ensued during the team's first meeting.
>
> **Teacher A:**   "If we can get *all* teachers to buy into teaching reading comprehension strategies in their classrooms, students will be exposed to strategies more often."
>
> **Teacher B:**   "We've tried that and there has not been a great deal of support. The problem is we have too many kids who can't be taught. They are reading below grade level. When they show up, they are not engaged and they don't complete their assignments but just getting them in the door is even a challenge. School is not their priority."
>
> **Teacher C:**   "I agree. I only had 15 out of 25 students show up for period four today. They just aren't motivated and without support from the parents, it's out of my hands."
>
> **Teacher A:**   "So what is our plan? What are we going to suggest to the staff to improve reading comprehension scores?"
>
> **Teacher C:**   "Let's get back to basics and water down the curriculum!"
>
> In this example, the team attributes failure to external causes—mainly the students and their situations.

> Ashton High School just received its results from the state's annual literacy test. Although they had experienced small but incremental gains over the past 2 years, this year their scores declined slightly, placing them below the state average. A team of teachers have been asked to examine the scores and determine what steps to take to ensure that all students are successful in the next administration of the test. The school has a large population of students with free and reduced lunch and a disproportionate percentage of students with special education needs compared to other schools in the area. The sense of perceived collective teacher efficacy among the Ashton High School is very strong. Following are excerpts from the dialogue that ensued during the team's first meeting.

> **Teacher A:** "It's unfortunate that our scores declined this year. The staff will be disappointed. It wasn't due to our efforts. We all worked really hard and offered a ton of extra support to students. We'll have to figure out what else we can do to support students."
>
> **Teacher B:** "Yes, we still have a long way to go. The tutoring program was pretty successful, and we have data to support its impact. I think we need to get that back in place by next week."
>
> **Teacher C:** "I agree, and when we surveyed the students last year, they indicated that they found the Homework Helpline and feedback based on the practice test really helpful. The problem was that we weren't able to give everyone feedback and, for those who did receive it, it was a month after they wrote the practice test. If we can put a system in place to ensure students get more timely feedback, then that would be good."
>
> **Teacher A:** "I read an article last week about close reading. I wonder if we share it with the staff at the next staff meeting. It's a simple strategy that I think people would be willing to try."
>
> In this example, the team attributes failure to internal causes—mainly the team's improvement strategies.

Causal Attributions

Human beings perceive and attribute various causes when considering factors that contribute to their success and/or failure. Attributions can be internal or external. From a student's perspective, two main internal sources of attribution are effort and ability. A student might attribute success and/or failure to how much time she studied for a test. On the other hand, she may think it was her ability (or lack of ability) to master complex ideas that led to her success and/or failure. Teachers also make causal appraisals when it comes to students' successes and failures. These causal appraisals are also attributed to either internal factors or external factors. External attributions include influences from the home (e.g., family structure), the curriculum (e.g., arts programs, extracurricular programs, whole language programs, etc.), and the school (e.g., class size, open versus traditional classrooms, etc.). Since in this case, the cause is being appraised by the *teacher*, external factors would also include influences from the student (e.g., student's effort, ability, prior achievement, attitude, etc.). Internal attributions, from a teacher's perspective, include an appraisal of *his* or *her* ability and effort.

When teachers attribute students' successes and failures to internal factors rather than external factors, they in turn, believe their actions impact

<u>student achievement.</u> Collective efficacy is related to causal attributions of student outcomes. Staffs who are inefficacious attribute their failures to lack of ability. They believe they are not capable of meeting the needs of their students. On the other hand, when staffs see themselves as highly efficacious, they ascribe failure to their use of insufficient strategies and/or not enough effort. Bandura (1993) noted that "causal attributions affect motivation, performance, and affective reactions mainly through beliefs of self-efficacy" (p. 128). Groups act on their beliefs about what they can accomplish as well their beliefs about the likely outcomes of their performance. When staffs lack a sense of collective efficacy, they do not pursue certain courses of action because they feel they lack the capabilities to achieve positive outcomes.

Another way in which teachers' sense of efficacy is related to causal attributions of student outcomes is that "teachers with high sense of efficacy are more willing to take responsibility for student successes and failures than teachers who score low on teaching efficacy measures" (Georgiou, Christou, Stavrinides, & Panaoura, 2002, p. 585). Georgiou et al. (2002) noted that "teachers' causal attributions of their students' successes and failures are very important, since they

> "People infer high self-efficacy from successes achieved through minimal effort on difficult tasks, but they infer low self-efficacy if they had to work hard under favorable conditions to master relatively easy tasks." (Bandura, 1986, p. 402)

influence students' own attributions through teacher behavior" (p. 584). Furthermore, the authors noted that "attributions make a major contribution to the forming of expectancies that teachers hold for students' future academic success" (p. 584). Readers will learn more about expectancy effects in Chapter 2.

Goddard et al. (2000) noted that "the major influences on collective teacher efficacy are assumed to be the attributional analysis and interpretation of the four sources of information— mastery experience, vicarious experience, social persuasion, and affective state" (p. 486). The authors explained that organizations focus attention on the teaching task and teaching competence and assess those two areas in terms

> "[T]he attributional analysis and interpretation of mastery experiences, vicarious experiences, social persuasion, and affective states constitute processes through which the organization assesses the teaching task and faculty competence" (Goddard et al., 2000, p. 503). Perceptions of collective efficacy are formed when teachers weigh analysis of the teaching tasks and perceptions of group competence in relation to one another.

of organizational capacity to succeed in teaching students. Collective efficacy beliefs are shaped based on this assessment.

IN CONCLUSION

To influence collective efficacy beliefs, it is important for leaders to understand that several factors are at work in shaping beliefs. School leaders should be cognizant of these factors and nurture them. These factors are revisited and examined throughout this book. Ways to foster collective efficacy beliefs are outlined in Chapter 3, and explicit connections regarding professional learning designs that help shift casual attributions from external sources to internal sources are made throughout Chapter 4. Opportunities for building efficacy through mastery and vicarious experiences are also shared.

In the next chapter, research that demonstrates the productive teaching behaviors that are positively associated with teacher efficacy is shared. Student achievement is improved through the collective actions of teachers. Highly efficacious staffs are characterized by high expectations, effort, and persistence in overcoming the most difficult challenges. Teachers utilize more student-centered teaching approaches, are more open to change, and are willing to undertake challenging activities. Parental participation is more likely to be encouraged, and teachers are more committed to the school as an organization.

2 Consequences of Collective Teacher Efficacy

Efficacy expectations are a major determinant of people's choice of activities. (Bandura, 1977, p. 194)

The strength of collective efficacy beliefs affects how school staffs tackle difficult challenges. Collective beliefs about the staffs' efficacy to motivate and promote learning affect the types of learning environments created in schools and the teaching behaviors exhibited by staff. When a sense of collective efficacy is present, staffs maintain school environments in which students feel good about themselves. They also engage in more productive behaviors that support positive student outcomes. When collective efficacy is not present, however, it takes a stressful toll on the staff. Kanter (2006) described lack of efficacy and resignation as reasons organizations are unable to solve problems.

Turning attention to improving collective teacher efficacy would be advantageous based on its impressive list of positive consequences. Ranking as the greatest influence impacting student achievement (Hattie, 2016) is no doubt related to the productive teaching behaviors and types of learning environments that are positively associated with teacher efficacy. These include (a) putting forth greater effort and persistence, especially aimed toward students experiencing difficulty; (b) trying new teaching approaches based on effective pedagogy; (c) conveying high expectations to students (teacher expectations); (d) fostering learner autonomy (student-centered teaching); (e) decreasing disruptive behavior; (f) increased commitment; and (g) enhanced parental involvement. Table 2.1 displays the effect sizes of some of the positive consequences that result from a sense of collective efficacy discussed in this chapter. Research that supports the notion that these productive consequences result from teacher efficacy is shared as well.

Table 2.1 Productive Consequences Associated With Teacher Efficacy and Their Effect Size

INFLUENCE	EFFECT SIZE
Self-reported grades/student expectations	1.44
Student-centered teaching	0.54
Goals	0.50
Parental involvement	0.49
Self-concept	0.47
Teacher expectations	0.43
Time on task	0.38
Decreasing disruptive behavior	0.34

Source: Adapted from Hattie, J. (2012). *Visible learning for teachers: Maximizing impact on learning.* New York, NY: Routledge.

GREATER EFFORT AND PERSISTENCE

A staff's collective sense of efficacy enables teams to undertake challenging activities and persist with high-needs students, because they judge the staff is capable of meeting students' needs. Ross and Bruce (2007) noted that "teacher efficacy influences student achievement through teacher persistence" (p. 51) and highly efficacious teachers "view student failure as an incentive for greater teacher effort" (p. 51). Goddard, Hoy, and Woolfolk Hoy (2000) also noted that "collective teacher efficacy beliefs influence the level of effort and persistence that individual teachers put forth in their daily work" (p. 502). Lower collective efficacy leads to less effort, an inclination to stop trying, and lower levels of performance. Tschannen-Moran and Barr (2004) noted that "school staffs with high collective teacher efficacy display persistence and resiliency when working with students who are having difficulty improving achievement levels" (p. 194). Ross and Bruce (2007) noted that when collective efficacy is high, teachers attend more closely to the needs of students who are not progressing well. Finally, Ashton and Webb (1986) also found that when collective efficacy is high, teachers are less critical of students who make mistakes and work longer with students who have difficulty.

WILLINGNESS TO TRY NEW APPROACHES

When efficacy is high, teachers are more accepting of change and more likely to try new teaching approaches (Ross & Bruce, 2007) based on effective pedagogy. In addition to spending a high proportion of time on task (Wang, Haertel, & Walberg, 1993), they create more mastery instructional strategies for their students (Tschannen-Moran & Barr, 2004) and set more challenging goals (Allinder, 1994). When a strong sense of efficacy is present, students are afforded greater opportunities for successful performance accomplishments. These mastery experiences help build students' sense of academic efficacy. Challenging goals are set, and strong commitments to accomplish them are maintained. When teachers have greater self-efficacy, they work harder to design mastery experiences and that in turn increases students' self-efficacy.

CONVEYING HIGH EXPECTATIONS

Hattie's (2012) research showed that teacher expectations have an effect size of 0.43 (see Table 2.1), which means they are a powerful influence on the success of student learning. Hattie (2009) also noted, however, "The question is not 'Do teachers have expectations?' but 'Do they have false and misleading expectations that lead to decrements in learning or learning gains?'" (p. 121). To understand how teachers' expectations (high versus low) might influence student learning and students' expectations (which are a more powerful influence on the success of a student than the teacher's expectations), it is helpful to be aware of two forms of self-fulfilling prophecies—the Pygmalion Effect and the Golem Effect.

When teachers expect their students to perform at high levels, they do, as demonstrated in a 1963 experiment by Rosenthal and Jacobson. In Rosenthal and Jacobson's experiment, teachers were told that certain students would show surprising intellectual gains during the school year based on their results on the Harvard Test of Inflected Acquisition (when in fact this test did not exist and the children designated to show gains were randomly selected). Eight months later, children from whom the teacher had been led to expect intellectual gains actually showed significantly greater gains than did the other students—although the only difference was in the teacher's mind

Rosenthal and Fode (1963) first demonstrated the phenomenon of expectancy effects, in the context of a controlled laboratory research setting, testing the performance of rats running in a maze. When experimenters were led to expect that rats, who had been genetically bred for "maze-brightness," would show better performance than the "maze-dull" rats, they did. It was suggested that experimenters who expected better performance handled their rats more frequently and compassionately than did the experimenters who expected less.

(Rosenthal & Jacobson, 1968). Since Rosenthal and Jacobson's study, many researchers have focused on the relationship between teachers' expectations and student learning, reaching similar conclusions (Brophy, 1983; Brophy & Good, 1970; Rosenthal & Babad, 1985; Weinstein, 2002).

This self-fulfilling prophecy, whereby high expectations lead to an increase in performance, is known as the Pygmalion Effect. The phenomenon is named after the Greek myth of Pygmalion, a sculptor whose love brought to life a statue he carved. If teachers think students are in a top performing group (even if they were placed there randomly), teachers are likely to treat those particular students as high achievers, and as a result, student performance improves. Rosenthal and Babad (1985) found that "teachers tend to treat more favorably and obtain superior performance from students for whom they have more favorable expectations" (p. 38).

Figure 2.1 demonstrates how teachers' beliefs influence their actions toward students, which, in turn, impact students' beliefs about their own ability. As outlined in Table 2.1, the effect size of the expectations a student has about his or her own success is 1.44 (Hattie, 2012). This is second only to collective teacher efficacy in regard to factors that influence student achievement. Hattie (2009) noted that "these expectations of success (which are sometimes set lower than students could attain) may become a barrier for some students as they may only perform to whatever expectations they already have for their ability" (p. 44).

In the book titled *Confidence*, Kanter (2006) draws on lessons about people and how they work together (or do not work together) to produce better (or worse) results. Kanter (2006) noted that when we assume that people are capable concrete things happen that translate expectations into investments of resources or effort that actually improves performance. "Thinking that someone is a potential high performer encourages leaders and colleagues to look more closely at her, to invest more time, to pass on more tips, to find the positives that surely must be there and mention them, ignoring the negatives because surely they cannot be true" (p. 40).

Figure 2.1   The Pygmalion Effect

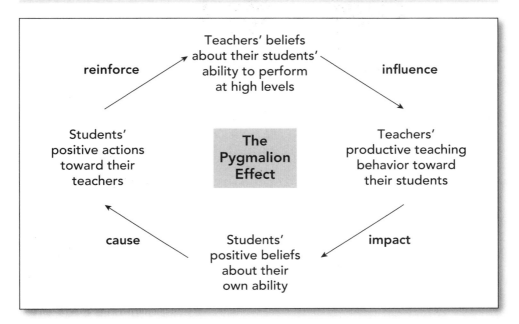

A self-fulfilling prophecy also occurs when teachers hold low expectations toward students. Low expectations lead to decreased performance. Also named after a mythical creature brought to life by its creator, this phenomenon is known as the Golem Effect. Unfortunately, Golem was rebellious, grew out of control, and as a result had to be destroyed. Teachers with low expectations produce behaviors that negatively impact the performance of their students while the students themselves produce negative behaviors. When teachers hold low expectations they employ inconsistent behavior toward low expectation students, including less wait time for students to respond and rewarding incorrect answers (Brophy, 1983).

> Graham (1990) suggested that at times, students gain attributional information about the causes of their behavior from teachers' affective displays. In addition, the communication of pity and/or offering of unsolicited help might send messages to students that they are incompetent and/or incapable.

In *The Water Is Wide: A Memoir*, Pat Conroy (2009) shared his experiences teaching fifth through eighth grade on Yamacraw Island. Yamacraw, located not far from Savannah, Georgia, had a high African American population. Their living depended on fishing and farming in the late 1960s.

Conroy shared the challenges he faced, including what he learned about his eighteen students in the first week: "Seven of my students could not recite the alphabet. Three children could not spell their names. Eighteen children thought Savannah, Georgia was the largest city in the world. Savannah was the only city any of the kids could name. Eighteen children had never seen a hill—eighteen children had never heard the words *integration* and *segregation*. Four children could not add two plus two. Two children did not know how old they were. Five children did not know their birthdates. Four children could not count to ten" (p. 36).

Conroy contrasts the different expectations held by him and Mama Brown, the only other teacher in the small school. On the first day of school Mama Brown addressed his class. Conroy recounts it as follows: "Most of you are slow," she said. "All of us know that. But there are two of you, Frank and Mary, who could take a test right now and move up a grade or two. That's because you got good brains and use them. The rest of you can't think as good. We know that and you know that. Your brains are just slow" (p. 26).

Despite the fact that Mama Brown had told Conroy the students were "retarded and not to waste time on them," after one month, Conroy reported that all the students could "present a reasonable facsimile of the alphabet upon request. They had also mastered the first ten numbers. They also recognized with varying degrees of success approximately thirty words" (p. 63).

He writes: "I then told them that they had to look upon themselves in a different light, that they had to be convinced of their basic worth, and that they could learn just as fast as anybody else" (p. 54).

Psychologists use the term *defensive pessimism* to describe the way some people lower expectations to cope with the anxiety arising from difficult situations. School staffs engaging in defensive pessimism lower their expectations to prepare themselves for failure when it comes to advancing the learning of hard-to-reach students. Kanter (2006) noted that "in real life—as in the sports teams, businesses, schools, and communities in my research—pessimism, whether defensive or not, is associated with excuses for failure, with denial of responsibility, and it serves as a self-fulfilling prophecy, even more than optimism does" (p. 108).

> *School staffs engaging in defensive pessimism lower their expectations to prepare themselves for failure when it comes to advancing the learning of hard-to-reach students.*

Rosenthal (1997) noted that effects of interpersonal expectations occur not only in classrooms but also in clinics, laboratories, workshops, sports, management, courtrooms, and nursing homes.

In *Sway: The Irresistible Pull of Irrational Behavior*, Brafman and Brafman (2008) shared examples of how the Pygmalion Effect and the Golem Effect played out in both the military and in psychiatry.

At an Israel training camp, 150 soldiers participated in a rigorous and intensive 15-week commander training program. Training officers were led to believe that soldiers had been previously placed in one of three "command potential" categories that included: high, regular, and unknown. At the end of the program, soldiers participated in a pencil and paper test that measured their new knowledge, and sure enough, the soldiers designated with high command potential scored significantly higher than the other soldiers.

The authors demonstrated how the mirroring of expectations occur using confirming examples from misdiagnosed psychiatric patients. For example, when a child who had been diagnosed as bipolar appeared tearful or upset, these emotions get interpreted as part of the condition. Brafman and Brafman (2008) noted that "the molding process becomes self-perpetuating: when we take on characteristics assigned to us, the diagnosis is reinforced and reaffirmed" (p. 100).

> In their study designed to predict susceptibility to bias, Rosenthal and Babad (1985) found that "not all teachers are equally susceptible to the biasing effects of interpersonal expectations" (p. 39). Readers are encouraged to raise their awareness of their susceptibility to bias.

In the recent past, I examined data from the Ontario Secondary School Literacy Test (OSSLT) from all secondary schools across the province of Ontario. While the overall results on the OSSLT reflected a third straight year of decline in 2012 (from 85% to 82% for successful first-time writers), the results for successful first-time writers enrolled in *applied* English courses were significantly lower than students enrolled in *academic* English and had declined more rapidly (from 62% to 53%) than the overall average over the same 4 years. Change efforts needed to focus on affecting positive changes in the outcomes for students studying at the applied level.

The purpose of the project was to identify schools that had obtained improved results regarding adolescent literacy achievement and examine classroom and leadership practices in each site in an effort to determine common components contributing to the achievement of students enrolled in applied level courses. Secondary schools, experiencing success for students enrolled in applied English courses, were identified based on the following criteria: (a) schools achieved an incremental increase in the success rate for first-time eligible (FTE) students enrolled in applied English over 4 or 5 years (2008–2012), and/or (b) schools maintained a success rate greater than 70% for FTE students enrolled in applied English for at least the previous 3 years.

Six schools were selected for interviews. Drawing from interview data from the six schools, powerful characteristics of successful, adaptable schools were

> identified. One of the themes, common and evident in each site, was that the staff and administration held high expectations for students' success. One team noted, "The message here is not 'turn it in and it's done—we're moving on.' The message is that students are expected to perform at the highest level possible so we provide opportunities for mastery learning. They know that we know they are capable of achieving at a high standard and therefore we expect them to do their best."

Expectations and Efficacy

When teachers are efficacious, they convey high expectations to their students (Bandura, 1997). When a school staff shares a sense of collective teacher efficacy, they convey high expectations to the student body. The opposite is true as well. The Golem Effect is also related to teachers' sense of efficacy because "students who are taught by teachers with a low sense of self-efficacy have lowered performance expectations" (Tschannen-Moran & Barr, 2004, p. 196). Students who are struggling academically will continue to experience difficulty if they receive instruction from teachers who have a weakened sense of efficacy (Bandura, 1997). Furthermore, when teachers lack efficacy beliefs, they weaken students' sense of efficacy (Bandura, 1993). Teachers with high expectations, on the other hand, convey to students that teachers hold the belief they can attain high levels of performance based on challenging and appropriate goals. As noted earlier, these beliefs result in self-fulfilling prophecies (Brophy & Good, 1970; Rosenthal & Jacobson, 1968). Students' self-concepts are improved when teachers hold high expectations.

Rubie-Davis, Hattie, and Hamilton (2006) brought to light an additional concern related to teachers' expectations with the finding that when teachers hold lower expectations, they do so for *all* students in the class. Perhaps readers have heard excuses that predict or explain poor performance such as: "Next year we'll have to deal with that really difficult group of students. You know the ones that are coming up. From what I hear, we can't expect much from that cohort. Our scores are sure to tank." Or "It was that weak group of students. You remember the group that year. They couldn't accomplish anything! That is why our scores were so low that year."

Given the fact that teachers' expectations powerfully influence student learning, coupled with the fact that teachers with a strong sense of efficacy convey high expectations while teachers with low efficacy beliefs convey low expectations, it makes sense to invest in fostering collective teacher efficacy as a school improvement strategy.

FOSTERING LEARNER AUTONOMY

One of the challenges of practice educators often grapple with is how to promote students' interest and enthusiasm in learning. How can educators equip students with the self-regulatory capabilities to be life-long learners? How can educators encourage the value students place on education? These outcomes are expressions of intrinsic motivation. Understanding the scientific research on intrinsic motivation including the significance of learner autonomy over learner control would be very beneficial for educators. Researchers have examined motivational teaching styles conceptualized along a continuum. One extreme is a student-centered classroom climate that supports autonomy and the other, a teacher controlled learning environment.

Student-centered classrooms move the focus from teaching to *learning* by providing students with greater autonomy. As outlined in Table 2.1, student-centered teaching has an effect size of 0.54 (Hattie, 2012). When students are provided with autonomy over their learning they are responsible for decisions regarding their learning and the implementation of those decisions. Students' interests drive the content. That does not mean that teachers disregard the curriculum or standards but, rather, they provide choice and set up learning opportunities that allow students to pursue their own interests and solve their own problems. Inquiry-based learning is one example. When students are provided autonomy they are allowed to share in the decision making by choosing the focus of content and how they demonstrate their learning. Students are provided the freedom to take charge of activities and control over learning processes. In a student-centered classroom, teachers create and maintain learning environments that support the development of student autonomy by providing scaffolds, encouraging peer support and cooperation, providing feedback, and empowering students.

In the book, *Why We Do What We Do: Understanding Self-Motivation*, Deci (1995) pointed out that autonomy support is a personal orientation that one takes toward other individuals. In the case of a teacher, this orientation would pervade all aspects of teaching and include the provision of choice for students. Deci (1995) noted that "part of being autonomy supportive means allowing individuals within your class or work group to participate in making decisions about issues that concern only them and part is sharing decision-making with the group as a whole" (p. 145). For example, if students must learn to read, the class would decide what to read and discuss how to make the decision—by majority, consensus, or by committee. Deci (1995) further acknowledged that there are limits and that curriculum has to be covered but pointed out that "there is almost always some room for deciding what to do" and "autonomy supportive teachers will accept the 'givens' and work with them" (p. 146).

Deci, along with his long-time collaborator and fellow researcher, Ryan, is well known for decades of research in this area. Ryan and Deci (2000) noted the "significance of autonomy versus control for the maintenance of intrinsic motivation has been clearly observed in studies of classroom learning" (p. 59). Ryan and Deci (2000) cite examples in which teachers who support student autonomy "catalyze in their students' greater intrinsic motivation, curiosity, and the desire for challenge" (p. 59). The authors also noted that when students are overly controlled, they lose initiative and learn less well, especially when learning is complex or requires conceptual, creative processing (Ryan & Deci, 2000).

In the book, *Drive: The Surprising Truth About What Motivates Us*, Pink (2009) noted that a sense of autonomy "has a powerful effect on individual performance and attitude" (p. 90). When individuals experience greater autonomy, intrinsic motivation increases, and when greater control is exerted over individuals, intrinsic motivation decreases (Pink, 2009). Zumbrunn, Tadlock, and Roberts (2011) noted that "intrinsic motivation and volition guide the level of effort and persistence" (p. 8) students use when completing assignments. Pink (2009) argued that "intrinsic motivation—the drive to do something because it is interesting, challenging, and absorbing" (p. 46)—is the "strongest and most pervasive driver [of learning]" (p. 23).

Motivation is also closely linked to competency beliefs and attributions. If students believe that they can successfully accomplish a particular task, they are more likely to select challenging tasks, stay with them longer, and perform better. In addition, when students attribute success to effort and strategy use, they start using better strategies (Dweck, 2008). Tough (2012) suggested that "in the last few years, economists, educators, psychologists, and neuroscientists have begun to produce evidence that developing non-cognitive skills such as persistence, self-control, curiosity, conscientiousness, grit, and self-confidence" (p. xv) is what matters most.

Learner Autonomy and Efficacy

Educators with high efficacy encourage student autonomy. Rather than exerting control over students, a student-centered teaching approach is valued. Woolfolk, Rosoff, and Hoy (1990) found that the stronger teachers believed that they could be successful, even with difficult and unmotivated students, the more the teacher supported student autonomy in solving problems. Teachers were "able to relinquish control and share responsibility for solving classroom problems with their students" (p. 146).

Leroy, Bressoux, Sarrazin, and Trouilloud (2007) also found that the more the teachers felt a sense of efficacy, "the more they reported that they reinforced students' needs for autonomy" (p. 538).

In the same study, Leroy et al. (2007) found that teachers with low self-efficacy provided less support for student individuality, conducting activities that were more controlling. Tschannen-Moran and Barr (2004) noted that "teachers who have a low sense of individual efficacy rely on extrinsic rewards and negative sanctions to motivate students" (p. 194). Hattie (2012) noted that extrinsic rewards lead to "greater shallow learning of surface features and completion of the work regardless of the standard and for the sake of praise or similar rewards" (p. 42).

Student outcomes including interest and enthusiasm in learning, self-regulation, and valuing education are expressions of intrinsic motivation. When educators foster student autonomy, intrinsic motivation increases. Given the fact that teachers with a strong sense of efficacy foster student autonomy and utilize student-centered approaches, it makes sense to focus on fostering collective teacher efficacy as part of a change strategy.

DECREASING DISRUPTIVE BEHAVIOR

Students display a wide range of behavior problems in schools including property destruction, physical aggression, disruptive talking in the classroom, and name calling on the playground. Disruptive behavior can have negative effects on the student's own and all other students' achievement. Dealing with the problem behavior is one of the most difficult aspects facing school staffs today. It can leave a staff feeling overwhelmed. It affects stress levels as well as teacher-student relationships and teacher-parent relationships. When considering its impact on student achievement, decreasing disruptive behavior has an effect size of 0.34 (Hattie, 2012).

Behavior and Efficacy

When collective efficacy is present, staffs are better equipped to foster positive behavior in students. Sorlie and Torsheim (2011) demonstrated that collective efficacy had a significant impact on student misconduct. The researchers noted that staffs with a strong sense of collective efficacy were "more likely to generate socially well-adapted students and to prevent and handle antisocial and rule-breaking behavior in more effective ways than school staffs with low confidence in their mutual capacity" (p. 187). Gibbs and Powell (2012) found that when teachers shared a collective belief in their efficacy for addressing the effects of external influences (home and community circumstances), they were ultimately less likely to exclude students from school as a consequence of their behavior. Studies show that teachers who expressed little belief in their efficacy were more likely to seek exclusion of problematic students from their classrooms. Klassen (2010) found that teachers' collective efficacy mediated the effects of stress from student behavior on job satisfaction.

Collective efficacy enhances teachers' ability to positively affect the behavior of all their students and influence what they choose to do as a group to meet misconduct. When collective efficacy is present, staffs are more likely to persist in their efforts to prevent and manage misbehavior. Staffs are also less discouraged by temporary setbacks and feel less stress resulting from student misbehavior. Whereas when collective efficacy is not present, staffs employ less uniform practice regarding behavior expectations and have a greater tendency to give up.

INCREASED COMMITMENT

The strength of the teaching profession depends on the degree of commitment of educators. Teacher commitment is a key factor influencing successful teaching. Committed staffs recognize their responsibilities to students and endeavor to fulfill them. Teacher commitment is a key to success in a school because a school's overall success in improving student achievement can only be fulfilled through teachers' active commitment to students in classrooms.

Commitment and Efficacy

Highly efficacious staffs show increased commitment and a willingness to exert effort on behalf of the organization (Lee, Zhang, & Yin, 2011). Ware and Kitsantas (2007) also found that collective efficacy beliefs predicted commitment to the teaching profession. This commitment was significantly related to teachers' influence regarding decision making at school. This idea is expanded on in Chapter 3 where school characteristics associated with collective efficacy are shared and ways to foster efficacy are presented.

ENHANCED PARENTAL INVOLVEMENT

Ranking as one of the greatest contributions related to the home, Hattie's (2012) research showed that parental involvement had an effect size of

0.49 (see Table 2.1). Hattie (2009) pointed out that there is much variance related to parental involvement depending on the type of approach (e.g., surveillance versus active approach) and when the involvement occurs (e.g., elementary school versus secondary school). Interestingly, in examining specific types of parental involvement and student achievement, Jeynes (2007) found that parental expectations (defined as the degree to which a student's parents maintained high expectations of the student's ability to achieve at high levels) had the greatest impact.

Parental Involvement and Efficacy

Enhanced teacher–parent relationships exist when staffs are highly efficacious. Ross and Gray (2006) found that collective teacher efficacy strongly predicted commitment to community partnerships and parental participation. When the staff was confident in their own abilities and effectiveness, they were more likely to welcome parental participation. Ross and Gray (2006) noted that "involving parents exposes teachers to such risk as negative feedback on school performance and identification of different goals and values than those identified by the school. A staff with high expectations that it will be able to overcome such obstacles is more likely to open itself to parental participation" (p. 192).

IN CONCLUSION

When a sense of collective efficacy is shared, teacher behaviors are favorable to actions that impact student results, including setting more challenging goals, increasing parental involvement and time on task, and decreasing disruptive behavior to name a few. At the same time, when efficacy is in doubt, teachers spend less time on academics and are more likely to give up on students who do not learn quickly. Clearly, efficacy matters. Fostering collective efficacy is a timely and important issue if we are going to realize success for all students. School characteristics associated with collective efficacy and ways to enhance collective efficacy are shared in the chapter that follows.

3 Fostering Collective Teacher Efficacy

The leader who helps develop focused collaborative capacity will make the greatest contribution to student learning. (Fullan & Quinn, 2016, p. 57)

Rather than leaving it to chance, it is timely and important to consider how collective efficacy beliefs may be fostered in schools and organizations. As noted earlier, given its effect on student achievement, fostering collective teacher efficacy should be a top priority and at the forefront of a planned strategic effort in all schools and school districts. Tschannen-Moran and Barr (2004) noted that the "success of the school, as indicated by levels of student achievement, depends upon the collective belief that the teachers in that building can improve student achievement" (p. 192). Perceptions of collective efficacy vary greatly among schools. Some staffs believe that through their collaborative efforts they can help students achieve in measurable ways, while others feel that they can do very little to impact student results. The adaptive challenge is in shifting the latter group's beliefs. While efficacy beliefs are not set in stone, they do require a concerted and substantial effort to change.

Six enabling conditions for collective teacher efficacy are shared in this chapter, and a theory of action for fostering collective efficacy is outlined. The theory includes four leadership practices that have a high likelihood of success. While there is no failsafe set of steps leaders can take, by both attending to the enabling conditions and adopting leadership practices outlined in the theory of action, change agents help build collective teacher efficacy. Questions for consideration and suggested small steps are included to help readers get started. Structures for professional learning, protocols, and practical strategies that will further assist leaders in moving from theory to practice are shared in Chapter 4.

The term *change agent* is used throughout this chapter and is intended to be all encompassing to include individuals at every level in the education system. Everyone, regardless of what position is held, has the ability to create change and possesses leadership qualities that can be cultivated. Often, classroom teachers neither recognize their role as informal leaders nor how critical their role is within the system. Whether individuals hold formal titles or not, the ideas and leadership practices suggested in this book can be applied by every educator in the system: administrators, coaches, department heads, directors, educational assistants, teachers, and superintendents.

In Chapter 2, the relationship between teachers' expectancy beliefs and resulting student outcomes is outlined. When we hold high expectations, people rise to the occasion. The same principle can be applied to the expectations we hold of our colleagues. By holding high expectations in people's ability to lead and affect change, individuals will begin to see themselves as agents of change. To cultivate the quality of leadership in every educator, we need to share the belief that everyone has the capacity to lead. When readers encounter the term *leader* throughout this book, they are encouraged to expand the definition beyond those who hold designated titles.

SIX ENABLING CONDITIONS FOR COLLECTIVE TEACHER EFFICACY

School characteristics associated with collective teacher efficacy, documented in the research, helped in identifying six enabling conditions for collective efficacy to flourish (see Figure 3.1). While enabling conditions do not *cause* things to happen, they increase the likelihood that things will turn out as expected. Attending to these six enabling conditions will help in realizing the possibility of collective teacher efficacy in schools.

Advanced Teacher Influence

There is a *clear* and *strong* relationship between collective efficacy and the extent of teacher leadership in a school (Derrington & Angelle, 2013;

Figure 3.1 Six Enabling Conditions for Collective Teacher Efficacy

1. Advanced teacher influence
2. Goal consensus
3. Teachers' knowledge about one another's work
4. Cohesive staff
5. Responsiveness of leadership
6. Effective systems of intervention

Goddard, 2002; Knobloch, 2007). Advanced teacher influence involves teachers assuming specific leadership roles and, along with that, the power to make decisions on school-wide issues. Lewis (2009) suggested that "with more opportunity to participate in school decision-making, teams build more mastery experiences in this type of decision making and experience social persuasion through colleagues' feedback" (p. 72).

> Ross, Hogaboam-Gray, and Gray (2004) found a "reciprocal relationship between teacher ownership of school processes and collective teacher efficacy" (p. 180).

Many leading educational experts, including Hargreaves and Fullan (2012), advocate for increasing teachers' power to make decisions on issues related to school improvement as part of an effective change strategy. When teachers are entrusted with the responsibility to make important decisions, they not only form a strong sense of collective efficacy, but they also feel empowered as well. When teachers' voices count in regard to designing curriculum, assessment, and professional learning, efficacy increases.

At Riverdale High School, the principal made room for teachers to take on leadership roles. One way was by providing them the opportunity to decide how to address students' concerns. After learning about a survey that allowed students to give input on school improvement issues, a teacher took the lead in organizing the administration of the survey and forming a team that would analyze the results and determine next steps. The survey explored topics such as student engagement, emotional health, physical health, safe schools, and risky behaviors. After learning that only 43% of students felt a sense of belonging at the school, the teachers determined that there was a need to ensure that more students felt valued and accepted by their peers and teachers.

Although the principal found it difficult at times not to interfere with the teachers' decisions, she provided them with autonomy and access to a budget that allowed them to meet occasionally and purchase resources they deemed fit. Part of the teachers' strategy included increasing student involvement in decision making because they had experienced the benefits themselves. One year later, when the survey was administered again, there was a 40% increase in the number of students who felt a sense of belonging at the school.

SMALL STEPS

Change agents can identify areas that might be considered for school improvement (e.g., school environment, delivery of curriculum, professional learning, collective efficacy, parental involvement, etc.) and begin to advocate for meaningful involvement from all stakeholders. Who are the stakeholders? How can they be afforded greater influence over important decisions?

Goal Consensus

Having a clear set of goals is important to the success of any endeavor—including school improvement. Setting measurable and appropriately challenging school goals helps educators achieve purposeful results—especially when the staff reaches consensus on which goals to set. Kurz and Knight (2003) found that consensus on school goals was a significant predictor of collective efficacy in their study, which examined the relationship between the two. A study undertaken by Leithwood and Sun (2009) demonstrated that by building consensus on goals, leaders had a significant positive impact on essential school conditions such as school culture, shared decision-making processes, teacher satisfaction, commitment, empowerment, and efficacy.

Bandura (1997) suggested that goal setting affected people's motivation, self-evaluation, and beliefs about the level at which they are capable of performing. Kurz and Knight (2003) pointed out that "both goal consensus and collective teacher efficacy have shared beliefs as a key element in their definitions" (p. 123). The authors further noted that "they differ in that collective teacher efficacy measures the perceptions that teachers have of their colleagues, while goal consensus measures the perceptions that teachers have regarding administrators and students, as well as the other teachers in that school" (p. 123).

In addition to impacting collective efficacy, reaching consensus on goals has a direct and measurable impact on student achievement. Robinson, Hohepa, and Lloyd (2009) synthesized the research that examined the impact of leadership dimensions on student outcomes and reported that goal setting had an effect size of 0.42. The authors defined goal setting in schools as "the setting, communicating and monitoring of learning goals, standards, and expectations and the involvement of staff and others in the process so that there is clarity and consensus about goals" (p. 95). Teachers need to have a voice in the process. When teachers actively participate in setting goals, they are more likely to pay attention to them as they helped in selecting them.

Chris, an instructional coach in an elementary school, used a protocol to help teachers reach consensus when determining goals and viable strategies for achieving them related to students' literacy learning. After identifying patterns in student work and determining metacognition was an area in which to focus, small teams created proposals outlining a plan of how to improve students' metacognition. Each team presented their proposal, which included a statement of the problem, rationale for their approach, strengths of the approach, challenges, and potential impact. After each presentation, Chris provided the larger group with the opportunity to ask clarifying questions. Rounds of warm and cool feedback followed before Chris gave the presenters an opportunity to respond to the feedback. A smaller group, which Chris referred to as *synthesizers*, discussed points of emerging consensus, possible areas of tension, and next steps before presenting them to the larger group. With a reminder that the goal was to build consensus, the larger group was given the opportunity to ask and answer new questions that emerged from the synthesis. Finally, Chris asked for volunteers to create a new plan that would incorporate the strengths and avoid the weaknesses outlined in the proposals presented. The groups' consensus-based plan was then presented, followed by a new round of warm and cool feedback. Although the protocol took time, Chris believed it was well worth it, indicating that as a result of the consensus building process, teachers felt ownership for the goals and the plan and thus were more likely to implement changes to their classroom practice than in the past.

SMALL STEPS

Leaders can help build collective efficacy by communicating a strong belief in the capacity of the staff to improve the quality of teaching and learning and attain appropriately challenging goals throughout the goal setting process. Acknowledge joint accomplishments. What small wins have resulted from team work?

Teachers' Knowledge About One Another's Work

It stands to reason that by gaining a more intimate knowledge of what goes on in other classrooms in the school, teachers' perceptions about the ability of their colleagues would be influenced. The question is: "Influenced in which direction?" One study noted that collective teacher efficacy was significantly associated with teacher knowledge of other teachers' courses (Newmann, Rutter, & Smith, 1989). While there are very few research studies that examined this relationship, one can't help but wonder about the moderating effects of various factors, including years of experience, professional development, teacher education programs, and subject-matter knowledge to name a few. If knowledge about one another's work develops via learning together collaboratively and a learning stance is assumed, then teachers could co-construct knowledge about effective teaching practices. Co-constructing new knowledge can be empowering and motivating and would likely lead to increased collective efficacy.

> Escobedo (2012) found that celebrations of success are perceived by teachers as positive events that strengthen their beliefs in the competence of the faculty.

SMALL STEPS

Change agents can set up opportunities for teachers to learn more about each other's work. Peer observation, videotaping instruction, teacher moderation, lesson study, developing common assessments, and the sharing teaching practices and student work are all ways in which teachers collaboratively learn and gain knowledge about their own and each other's practice. What opportunities are there for teachers to learn collaboratively?

Cohesive Staff

Cohesion is defined as the degree to which teachers agree with each other on fundamental and organizational issues (Fuller & Izu, 1986). School staff can hold unified or disparate beliefs about goal priorities, urgent student learning needs, promising instructional approaches, sound assessment strategies, and expectations about student performance. Ross et al. (2004) found that the more cohesive the staff, the more likely they are to give in to social persuasion. The authors believed the reason for this was because a cohesive staff was more likely to be aware of individual concerns. This awareness was used to construct persuasive arguments about the role individuals played in constituting an effective team. Ross et al.

(2004) further pointed out that the greater the cohesion, the more opportunities for teachers to see examples of successful collaborations, and this helped persuade teachers' perceptions regarding the efficacy of their colleagues. Ross et al. (2004) noted that when a staff is cohesive, the "social processes that generate peer support are likely to reduce effects of negative emotions on collective efficacy beliefs" (p. 167).

SMALL STEPS

Change agents build cohesion by speaking in terms of the team and encouraging individual teachers to think like a team. In addition to encouraging teachers to interact with each other whenever possible, clarify each teacher's role in achieving a common purpose as part of the larger team. In what ways are teachers interdependent on one another? What are some opportunities to increase interdependence?

Responsiveness of Leadership

In schools where leaders act consistently with the principle that it is their responsibility to help others carry out their duties effectively, leaders are responsive and show concern and respect for their staff. Responsive leaders demonstrate an awareness of the personal aspects of teachers and protect teachers from issues and influences that detract from their teaching time or focus. This includes providing teachers with materials and learning opportunities necessary for the successful execution of their job. When principals demonstrate the ability to respond to the needs of the staff, teachers feel supported and they have a greater belief in their collective ability to affect student outcomes. Staffs respond positively by working more diligently.

SMALL STEPS

Responsiveness requires awareness of situations—the details and undercurrents in the school. Is anything preventing the team from carrying out their duties effectively? If so, how can change agents respond to the situation in a way in which the team will feel supported?

Effective Systems of Intervention

It makes sense that in schools where effective systems of intervention are in place, staff would share a sense of collective efficacy. Effective interventions help ensure that *all* students are successful. Everyone plays an instrumental role in carrying out various aspects of the plan to ensure high levels of learning. As school staffs are instrumental in creating the conditions for success, they come to realize that through their collective efforts they can make a difference and help all students achieve.

A few years ago, I visited Adlai Stevenson High School and County Meadows Elementary School in the Kildeer Countryside School District 96 in Illinois. These schools are known for their success stories based on effective intervention systems. DuFour, DuFour, Eaker, and Karhanek (2010) wrote about both schools in *Raising the Bar and Closing the Gap: Whatever It Takes*. During the time I spent with staff, it was obvious that not only did they share a sense of collective responsibility, they also believed in their collective capability to ensure student success. DuFour et al. (2010) noted that "teachers in schools with effective systems of interventions and enrichment have a stronger sense of both self-efficacy and collective efficacy. It is not so much their perception of their students' abilities that creates a culture of high expectations in these schools, but their conviction regarding their own collective abilities to impact student achievement in a positive way" (p. 212).

SMALL STEPS

Change agents can strike up a task force to learn more about effective systems of intervention. The task: Evaluate aspects of intervention plans and determine which aspects might be transferable to their school environment. Collective efficacy is built through vicarious experiences.

Six enabling conditions, identified from research on school characteristics associated with collective teacher efficacy, were outlined above. By attending to the enabling conditions, change leaders increase the likelihood that collective efficacy will be fostered. Suggested small steps were offered, and additional insights will be gained through the theory of action that is outlined in the following section.

FOSTERING COLLECTIVE EFFICACY: A THEORY OF ACTION

By strengthening collective teacher efficacy, teachers will develop the resolve to persist against challenges and realize increased student results. Although there is still much to be learned regarding factors that contribute

Figure 3.2 A Theory of Action for Fostering Collective Teacher Efficacy

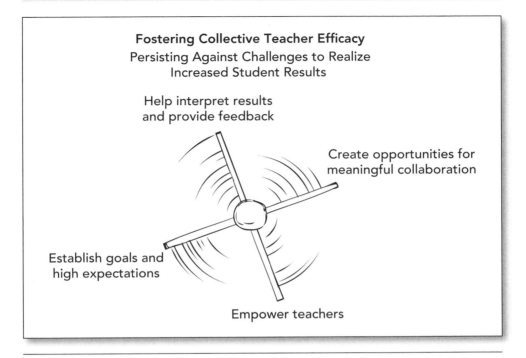

Source: Propeller image courtesy of erich007/iStock/Thinkstock.

to collective efficacy, existing research provides guidance on *leadership practices* that have a high likelihood of fostering efficacy. These leadership practices comprise the theory of action illustrated in Figure 3.2. Conceptualizing the theory involved an extensive review of the research literature. The theory is *fostering collective teacher efficacy* to *realize increased student achievement,* and it involves *creating opportunities for meaningful collaboration, empowering teachers, establishing goals and high expectations,* and *helping educators interpret results and provide feedback.*

Theories of action help expose thinking and are essential in clarifying visions for change. Bushe's (2010) *cardwork* strategy, shown in Figure 3.2, has been used to make the theory about fostering collective efficacy more explicit. The title describes what the theory is about, the subtitle articulates the outcomes of successful actions, and the phrases indicate a complete theory of how to reach that outcome. The purpose of the spinning propeller is to show that the critical aspects are not necessarily accomplished in a step-by-step sequence, but rather they *spin* to demonstrate a more fluid approach.

The theory includes the following leadership practices that have a high likelihood of success: (a) creating opportunities for meaningful collaboration, (b) empowering teachers, (c) establishing goals and high expectations, and (d) helping teams interpret results and provide feedback. There are a number of assumptions, however, embedded in these statements. The first assumption is that the collaboration will be meaningful—that is, avoiding the pitfalls that prevent groups from making good decisions and resulting in changes in thinking and behavior that lead to improvements in learning, teaching, and leading. A second assumption is that the collaboration will occur with enough frequency to foster teachers' sense of collective efficacy. There is an assumption that teachers want leadership opportunities and are willing to accept additional responsibilities. It is assumed that teachers will understand goals and be committed to them and that everyone shares a common understanding of the term *high expectations*. The final assumption is that the culture is one in which teachers are ready and willing to share student evidence, interpret results collectively, and receive and act on feedback. Each component in the theory of action is further expanded on in light of these assumptions.

Four Successful Leadership Practices

While there are a number of exemplary leadership practices highlighted in research, the four outlined here are considered highly effective in relation to developing collective teacher efficacy, based on a review of research literature. An overview of each practice is shared along with helpful information that will assist change leaders as they consider how they might enact each practice. Little's (1990) continuum of collegial relations is a useful framework when considering how to structure opportunities for meaningful collaboration. The Ladder of Teacher Involvement in School Decision Making is a useful tool when considering how to empower teachers. Understanding how goal setting works will help leaders create the conditions required for teams of teachers to set relevant and appropriately challenging goals. When interpreting evidence and providing feedback, the critical role change agents play is helping teachers identify cause-effect relationships. In addition, readers will also find a list of questions to consider regarding each leadership practice. Later in the book, readers are guided through an inquiry process as a way to further examine leadership practices aimed at strengthening the collective efficacy of their school staff.

Teachers are often asked to examine aspects of their practice for the purpose of improving student learning. Just as the practice of teaching can be examined, the practice of leadership can be studied as well. Change agents are encouraged not only to consider the suggestions in this chapter and put into practice the ones that seem contextually relevant and congruent with individual leadership styles and preferences, but to also monitor, reflect on, and learn from the practices. Evaluating the impact of various leadership practices and moves will not only help leaders in honing their craft, it will also help inform and strengthen strategic plans designed to foster collective efficacy. In the final chapter of this book, readers are guided through a cycle of inquiry as a means to reflect on and evaluate the impact of their moves.

Creating Opportunities for Meaningful Collaboration

Structures and processes need to be in place for educators to come together to solve problems of practice collaboratively. Teachers and administrators need time, during the instructional day, and spaces, conducive to learning, where they can meet regularly. Time in which to collaborate was an organizational factor found to contribute to increase efficacy (Newmann et al., 1989). Johnson (2012) set out to determine the frequency of collaboration time that was needed to significantly impact teachers' perceptions of collective efficacy and found that when teachers collaborated three or more times per week collective efficacy perceptions were significantly and positively affected.

The provision of time and the formation of teams, however, do not *guarantee* that collaboration will result in a sense of collective efficacy, changes in beliefs and practice, and/or increased student outcomes. There are pitfalls that occur as a result of groupthink. Katz, Earl, and Ben Jaafar (2009) identified "psychologically grounded dangers of the collective" (p. 8), including diffusion of responsibility and *sameness* trumping diversity. Hargreaves and Fullan (2012) also warned that "collaboration can be too warm and too cold" (p. 127) and described forms of collaboration that possess negative connotations, including balkanization and contrived collegiality.

In the book *Wiser: Getting Beyond Groupthink to Make Groups Smarter*, Sunstein and Hastie (2015) also shared distinct problems that occur when people get together to make decisions. The authors warned that groups fall victim to the *cascade effect*. This occurs when team members follow the statements and actions of whoever speaks or acts first—even if those statements or actions lead the team in the wrong direction. They also warned that groups often become more *polarized*, ending up in more extreme positions in line with tendencies of the individual group members. For example, a group of people, inclined toward cynicism, become excessively cynical as a result of team discussions. Finally, Sustain and Hastie (2015) noted that "groups focus on shared information—*what everybody knows already*—at the expense of unshared information and thus fail to obtain the benefit of critical information that one or a few people have" (p. 24).

Protocols help structure conversations in ways that helps teams maintain objectivity and focus. Protocols are simply an agreed upon set of guidelines that help ensure that collaboration time is used efficiently, productively, and purposefully. They are a useful way to avoid the pitfalls of groupthink. City, Elmore, Fiarman, and Teitel (2009) noted that the value of protocols "comes from making the rules of interaction explicit—they establish that the group is accountable to each other and they provide the means for facilitators and participants to hold a group to their agreements" (p. 76). A number of books are devoted to this topic. In addition, protocols that help foster collective efficacy are outlined in Chapter 4.

Continuum of Collegial Relations. In examining teacher teams and their contribution to the productivity of schools, Little (1990) noted that "closely bound groups are instruments both for promoting change and for conserving the present" (p. 509). Little (1990) distinguished forms of collegial relations to "account for the consequences felt in the classroom" (p. 512). Even though Little's (1990) continuum of collegial relations was developed more than 25 years ago, it is still a useful tool today for examining collaboration in schools.

At the bottom of the continuum, storytelling and scanning for ideas take place under conditions of nearly complete independence. Little (1990) noted that "teacher autonomy rests on freedom from scrutiny and the largely unexamined right to exercise personal preference; teachers acknowledge and tolerate the individual preferences or styles of others" (p. 513). At the next level, aid and assistance are described as help or advice seeking from one colleague to another. Questions asked are interpreted as requests for help, and therefore matters of teaching are treated in a piecemeal fashion and do not lead to deep discussions about the practice of teaching. Individualism is sustained because teachers do not interfere in each other's work in unwarranted ways. Examinations of practice are unlikely to result from these exchanges.

> Hattie (2015) noted that "too often, collaboration is about sharing resources, sharing anecdotes and war stories and sharing beliefs about why or why not something might work in 'my' context" (p. 23).

Little's (1990) third conception of collegiality, sharing, is based on the exchange of materials, methods, ideas, and opinions. "Through routine sharing, teaching is presumably made less private, more public" (p. 518). By making their materials accessible, teachers expose ideas and intentions and the groundwork is laid for productive discussion and debate regarding professional practice. It cannot be assumed, however, that through sharing teachers' day-to-day practice will be influenced. Finally, Little (1990) described joint-work as teacher's collective action and interdependence on each other. It is based on "teachers' decisions to pursue a single course of action in concert or, alternatively, to decide on a set of basic priorities that in turn guide the independent choices of individual teachers" (p. 519). Motivation to participate is based on the fact that each other's contributions are required to succeed in independent work. It includes the "joint deliberation over difficult and recurring problems of teaching and learning" (p. 520). Professional practices are examined publicly and open to scrutiny. Common understandings regarding effective practice are built collaboratively as a result.

In considering Little's (1990) continuum of collegial relations, clearly the goal is to move beyond storytelling and scanning for ideas and aid and assistance. Teachers need to be introduced to processes that support joint-work and aid in addressing challenges related to learning, leading, and

> "Groups are powerful, which means they can be powerfully wrong. Getting together without the discipline and specificity of collective deliberation can be a grand waste of time." (Fullan & Quinn, 2016, p. 13)

teaching. For collaboration to be productive, fostering collective efficacy, leading to changes in beliefs and practice and ultimately, increasing student achievement, it has to be purposefully organized. To reach the level of joint-work and to ensure teams avoid the pitfalls of groupthink, structures and processes need to be in place that promote and require interdependence, collective action, transparency, and group problem solving in search of a deeper understanding.

Federally funded grants and NCLB

QUESTIONS TO CONSIDER

Think about the teacher teams in your school.

- How often do teams come together? Are there opportunities to increase collaboration time?
- Do teams fall prey to the pitfalls of groupthink?
- Where is the team along the continuum of collegial relations?

  - Storytelling and scanning for ideas?
  - Aid and assistance?
  - Sharing?
  - Joint-work?

- What is the team's level of readiness to move toward joint-work? How can they be supported?
- To what degree is team work characterized by collective responsibility, collective action, interdependence, and group problem solving?

Empowering Teachers

When formal leaders provide opportunities for shared leadership by affording others the power to make decisions, everyone benefits. Teachers are empowered when they have a voice in school decisions. Decisions are better understood and more readily accepted. Change is more likely to be effective and lasting when those who implement it feel a sense of ownership and responsibility for the process. In addition, Goddard, Hoy, and Woolfolk Hoy (2004) noted that "where teachers have the opportunity to influence important decisions, they also tend to have stronger beliefs in the conjoint capability of their faculty" (p. 10).

Participative decision making represents a deliberate change from models based on hierarchy. Allowing teachers' equal voices on matters that have traditionally been determined by administrators can be an arduous endeavor. It requires risk-taking and a strong belief in empowerment over efficiency, choice over decisiveness, and autonomy over control. It also requires a great deal of patience and requires that administrators resist the temptation to offer advice and solve problems for their staff. It does not mean that principals remove themselves from all decisions, but rather they must become equal participants in the process. Although it might be challenging at times to not override teachers' decisions, it is an important aspect in fostering collective efficacy.

Teacher Involvement in Decision Making. There are varying degrees of involvement in school decision making. Simply inviting participation does not *guarantee* that teachers will feel empowered or an increased sense of collective efficacy. Teachers will experience feelings of alienation or empowerment based on their perception of the scope of their influence. Teachers will feel less empowered (perhaps even disempowered) if they perceive their influence as low. Teachers will feel a greater sense of engagement and increased efficacy if they perceive their influence as high. The Ladder of Teacher Involvement in School Decision Making (Figure 3.3) outlines varying degrees of teacher involvement. The higher up one moves on the ladder of involvement, the greater the influence.

Figure 3.3 Ladder of Teacher Involvement in School Decision Making

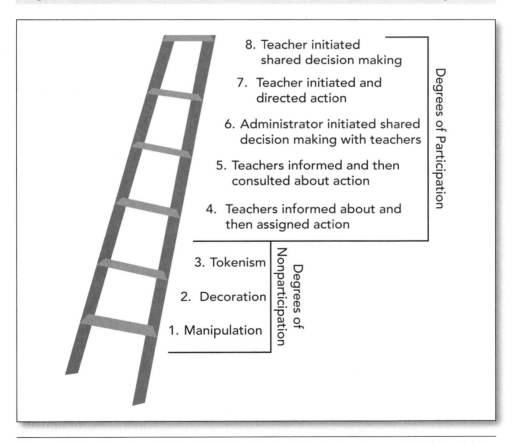

8. Teacher initiated shared decision making

7. Teacher initiated and directed action

6. Administrator initiated shared decision making with teachers

5. Teachers informed and then consulted about action

4. Teachers informed about and then assigned action

Degrees of Participation

3. Tokenism

2. Decoration

1. Manipulation

Degrees of Nonparticipation

Source: Modified based on Fletcher, A. (2003). *Meaningful student involvement: Guide to inclusive school change.* Retrieved from https://soundout.org/wp-content/uploads/2015/07/MSI_Guide_to_ Inclusive_School_Change.pdf; adaptation of Hart, R. A. (1992). Children's participation: From tokenism to citizenship. *Innocenti Essays, 4.* Retrieved from https://www.unicef-irc.org/publications/pdf/ childrens_participation.pdf

Degrees of Nonparticipation (1 Being the Lowest)

1. **Manipulation:** Formal leaders use teachers to support causes by falsely claiming those causes are inspired by the staff.

2. **Decoration:** Teachers are used to help bolster a cause in a relatively indirect way. Formal leaders do not pretend that the causes are inspired by teachers. Causes are determined by formal leaders and leaders make all the decisions.

3. **Tokenism:** Teachers appear to be given a choice but in fact have little or no choice about what they do or how they participate.

Degrees of Participation (8 Being the Highest)

4. **Assigned but taught:** Teachers are assigned specific roles but are told how and taught why they are being involved.

5. **Consulted and informed:** Teachers give advice on projects or school-wide activities owned and run by formal leaders. Teachers are informed about how their input will be used, but the outcomes are based on decisions made by formal leaders.

6. **Administrator initiated decisions shared with teachers:** Projects, school-wide activities, and school improvement processes are initiated by formal leaders, but the decision making is shared with teachers involved.

7. **Teacher initiated and directed:** Teachers initiate and direct projects and school-wide activities, including professional learning and strategies for school improvement. Administrators are involved in a supportive role.

8. **Teacher initiated, but shared decision making with administrators:** Projects and school-wide activities are initiated by teachers, and decision making is shared among formal and informal leaders. Teachers design and lead professional learning and school improvement strategies. These projects empower teachers while at the same time allowing them to access and learn from experience and the experiences of others.

Teacher participation in decision making heightens commitments to decisions made and motivation to carry them out—the greater the degree of participation, the greater the influence. Successful influence improves efficacy. When staffs successfully influence decisions and believe in their collective ability to successfully carry out those decisions, a sense of collective efficacy is fostered. One of the assumptions identified in the theory of action about fostering collective efficacy was that teachers want leadership opportunities and are willing to accept additional responsibilities. The feeling of empowerment that comes from successful influence not only enhances efficacy, but it also results in an increased engagement and a desire to be involved.

Have you ever experienced nondegrees of participation while serving on a committee?

I think we all have. I recall conversations with some of my friends who are also educators. I asked a principal once why he no longer participated on a school district's Character Education Committee. His response, "It is Veronica's show. She does all the talking and rarely asks for our input. We're just there on paper."

Another friend shared an experience she had while serving on a school district's committee responsible for interviewing and hiring for positions of added responsibility. She decided to no longer accept the invitation to take part. When I asked her why, she replied, "The decision was already made. Even if the committee unanimously votes for a different candidate, the superintendent gets who she wants in the end. When she tries to convince us to change our vote, we all cave under the pressure. Our voices don't really count."

Another colleague was invited to participate on a planning committee to help design the agenda for a national organization's annual meeting. After the agenda was developed, the lead consulted the planning committee. During the annual meeting, the audience was informed that the role of the planning committee was to represent their voices in designing a purposeful agenda. My colleague told me that in fact there was very little consultation. She was basically assigned a small, predetermined role to play during the meeting. She had ideas about how to better meet the needs of the audience but was never given an opportunity to share her ideas or voice her concerns. This is a fine example of tokenism.

QUESTIONS TO CONSIDER

Think about the teacher teams in your school. Regarding involvement in school decision making:

- What is the current degree of participation for teacher teams?
- Are there opportunities to increase the involvement of teacher teams in decision making?

(Continued)

(Continued)

- What are teachers' perceptions regarding their scope of influence?
  - Do they feel empowered?
  - Do they feel alienated?
  - Or somewhere in between?

- How can the discrepancy between current and preferred levels of participation be addressed?
- Think of a time you experienced nondegrees of participation while serving on a committee. What was the experience and what did it feel like?
- Think of a time you experienced a much greater degree of participation while serving on a committee. What was the experience, and what did it feel like?

Establishing Goals and High Expectations

Establishing goals and high expectations is highlighted in the research on effective leadership practices. In the book *Flow: The Psychology of Optimal Experience*, Csikszentmihalyi (1990) noted the optimal state of inner experience happens when our attention is invested in realistic and clear goals. Few would argue that the notion of setting and communicating clear goals based on high expectations is important to the success of a school or district's strategic plan. Most would also acknowledge that it takes a special skill set to lead a group in collaboratively developing, communicating, and gaining consensus on powerful goals that transform learning, teaching, and leading. Understanding why goal setting is important and having knowledge of how goal setting works is critical to the effective execution of this leadership practice.

How Goal Setting Works. Based on a synthesis of 31 research studies, Robinson et al. (2009) demonstrated how goal setting works (see Figure 3.4). The authors identified three conditions that must be met in setting goals. The conditions of effective goal setting required that (1) the team had the capacity to meet the goals, (2) the goals were clear and specific, and (3) the staff was committed to the goals. In addition to the conditions required, the authors also outlined the processes involved and consequences of effective goal setting. When there is a discrepancy between a school's current situation and their desired future, the dissatisfaction experienced by the staff motivates them to take action to close the gap—as long as they are

Figure 3.4 How Goal Setting Works

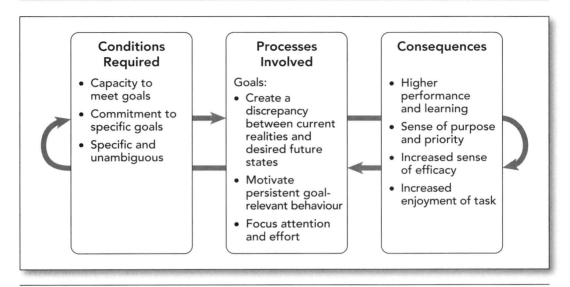

Source: Adapted from Robinson, V., Hohepa, M., & Lloyd, C. (2009). *School leadership and student outcomes: Identifying what works and why.* Best evidence synthesis iteration [BES]. Auckland: New Zealand Ministry of Education.

committed to the goal. In addition to consensus on school goals being a significant predictor of collective teacher efficacy (Kurz & Knight, 2003), goals help in focusing the staff's attention and result in determination and sustained effort. Performance and learning are enhanced. Psychological benefits include greater enjoyment of the staff's work and greater willingness to take on challenges. These benefits result from a sharper sense of purpose.

"Leaders establish the importance of goals by communicating how they are linked to pedagogical, philosophical, and moral purposes. They gain agreement that the goals are realistic and win collective commitment to achieving them." (Robinson et al., 2009, p. 40)

Additional insights regarding setting goals that were gleaned from Robinson et al.'s (2009) synthesis included evidence indicating that

- an effective way for leaders to establish the importance of goals was to link the goals to a wider and moral purpose;
- perceived difficulty of a goal changed as the staff's capacity changed—therefore it was important for leaders to work with staff in setting progressively more challenging goals; and
- the level of staff consensus on school goals was a significant discriminator between otherwise similar, high- and low-performing schools.

> "People with high self-efficacy set their goals high, because they are not satisfied with less." (Latham & Locke, 2006, p. 332)

School teams can overcome the gap between their school's current situation and desired future. A key to their success is in establishing and maintaining high expectations for *all* students. Change agents are encouraged to view school goals through the lens of high expectations. As part of an ongoing reflection process, leaders must engage staff in considering and combating negative influences of messages of lowered expectations. In addition, leaders must ensure that staffs share a common understanding of the term *high expectations*.

Lisa, a seventh-grade teacher, came to realize that she and her colleague, Michael, had very different ideas about what holding students to high expectations meant. When discussing high expectations, Michael stated the following: "I hold my students to high expectations. I expect them to complete their homework on time. I expect them to keep their notebooks neat and titles underlined and I expect them to always be prepared for class." While Lisa agreed that the work habits Michael described were important, her ideas about holding high expectations centered on her belief that her students could comprehend difficult texts, master complex content, and were capable of solving challenging problems.

QUESTIONS TO CONSIDER

Based on Robinson et al.'s (1990) conceptualization of how goal setting works

- Has your team met the conditions required?
- How will you ensure the staff is sufficiently motivated to take action?

Think about the goals set by teacher teams in your school.

- What is the wider and moral purpose of the goals?
- How would the goals articulated by the team read if written at a classroom level by an individual teacher? By a student?
- How do the goals apply to different subsets in the school population?

  ○ Are they sufficiently robust for subsets?
  ○ Are the expectations high for all groups?

Helping Teams Interpret Results and Provide Feedback

To know what kind of an impact teachers are having on students, information is needed to help identify challenges of practice and track progress. To interpret results, teachers must examine evidence of student learning. The examination of evidence is not an end in itself but rather a means to improve decisions in schools and in classrooms. Teachers need time to acquire skills, a clear purpose, and support when interpreting evidence. The critical role change agents play is in helping teachers identify cause-effect relationships. Reeves (2010) noted that in systems where cause and effect data are examined and the link between the actions of teachers and student results is documented in a clear and public way, replication of mistakes is unlikely.

Interpreting results by examining student learning data helps strengthen connections between the learning task, content, instruction, and student outcomes.

> *The critical role change agents play is in helping teachers identify cause-effect relationships.*

The aim is to shift conversations from generalized talk about student's progress and polite sharing of teaching strategies to more in-depth conversations about the connections between the two (Nelson, Deuel, Slavit, & Kennedy, 2010). Teachers are often concerned that the process will surface questions related to professional expertise and therefore might be a big hurdle for some school staffs.

In regard to helping teams interpret results, Hattie (2012) noted the "most successful method" (p. 60) involved small teams of teachers meeting every 2 to 3 weeks using an "explicit, data-driven structure to disaggregate data, analyze student performance, set incremental goals, engage in dialogue around explicit and deliberate instruction, and create a plan to monitor student learning and teacher instruction" (p. 60). In Chapter 4, a collaborative inquiry framework that involves the collective examination of student learning data in light of changes in instructional practice is shared. "The collaborative inquiry cycle necessitates ongoing conversations and reflection among participants focused on assessing the impact of their actions on student learning" (Donohoo & Velasco, 2016, p. 53).

Filbin (2008) examined the impact of changes in data-driven teaching and leading on collective efficacy. The researcher found a "direct and significant impact on collective efficacy when teachers reported higher uses of data to change instruction" (p. 158). Collective efficacy beliefs were elevated as teachers increased their use of data to be instructionally responsive to their student learning needs.

Hattie noted that "the evidence of enhanced impact feeds efficacy" (personal communication, August 2016).

The interpretation of results, which is part of the inquiry cycle, leads to shifts in causal attributions, a source of efficacy described in Chapter 1. Protocols for examining evidence are outlined as well. Protocols will help ensure team members feel safe in publicly sharing student results as they build objectivity into conversations.

QUESTIONS TO CONSIDER

Think about the teams in your school.

- How often do teams come together to interpret results?
- Do teams receive feedback about their impact on student learning?
- How do teams respond to that feedback?
- What opportunities are provided for collaborative analysis of student work?

IN CONCLUSION

From the research on school characteristics associated with collective teacher efficacy, six enabling conditions for fostering efficacy were identified (see Figure 3.1). This chapter also outlined four leadership practices that can be adopted in an effort to prioritize actions and increase the likelihood of success.

The context of change must be at the collective level rather than the individual level. It is important that change agents create opportunities for meaningful collaboration. Hattie (2015) noted "there is no way that a system will make an overall difference to student achievement by working one teacher at a time" (p. 5). Hargreaves and Fullan (2012) noted that "teaching like a pro is not about yet more individual accountability, but about powerful collective responsibility" (p. 23). To support collective learning, structures and processes need to be in place to help teams move beyond "happy talk" (Sunstein & Hastie, 2015) and avoid the pitfalls that occur when people come together to make decisions as a group.

"Professionals understand the power of the team, promote the development of the team, and become integral parts of the team themselves." (Hargreaves & Fullan, 2012, p. 23)

Teachers also need to be empowered and provided with experiences to grow as leaders. Empowerment is also referred to as *shared decision making*. The more teachers have the opportunity to influence school improvement decisions, the more likely the school will be characterized by a robust sense of collective efficacy (Goddard et al., 2004). Not only is efficacy and leadership capacity built through participation in decision making, instructional capacity increases as well. Insights regarding goal setting were shared. High expectations should be reflected in goals created. Leaders need to set the conditions so that teachers feel the discrepancy between the current and desired states. The feelings created by the discrepancy will motivate teachers to take action. Furthermore, when teams interpret performance results and are provided with feedback about their performance, educators come to identify and build on specific efforts and the mastery and vicarious experiences that resulted in success. Confidence and collective efficacy are nurtured when reasons for success are identified and attributed to the collective efforts of the staff.

As noted earlier, collective efficacy beliefs are malleable; however, they require a concerted and substantial effort to change. Goddard, Hoy, and Woolfolk Hoy (2000) noted that once developed there is reason to believe that collective teacher efficacy will thrive. While there is no failsafe set of steps change leaders can take, they can attend to the six enabling conditions for collective efficacy and adopt the four promising practices described in this chapter to help foster collective teacher efficacy. Professional learning structures, protocols, and other practical strategies that require interdependence and build cohesion are shared in Chapter 4. Implementing these powerful designs will help ensure teachers' collegial encounters are grounded in joint-work and empower teachers while fostering collective efficacy.

4 Enhancing Collective Efficacy Through Professional Learning

Effective change processes shape and reshape good ideas as they build capacity and ownership among participants. (Fullan & Quinn, 2016, p. 14)

When educators engage in continuous learning, student learning is improved. As members of a teaching profession, it is incumbent upon us to continuously learn and improve our practice throughout our career. Educators continue to develop the knowledge and skills needed to address adaptive challenges through professional learning. Collective efficacy can also be developed through professional learning. Therefore, it is important to understand the significance of collective efficacy when planning for professional learning.

While the importance of continuous improvement is recognized, opportunities for educators to engage in meaningful professional learning are not yet commonplace. "Significant variation in both support and opportunity for professional learning exists among schools and states" (Darling-Hammond, Wei, Andree, Richardson, & Orphanos, 2009, p. 5).

Enhancing collective efficacy through professional learning remains a challenge. Unfortunately, some school districts continue to rely heavily on models of professional development that neither meet the learning needs of educators nor provide efficacy shaping experiences. In addition, transfer to practice is unlikely given traditional professional development designs.

Darling-Hammond et al. (2009) examined the nature of professional development opportunities available to teachers across the United States and abroad. A few of the key findings included that most teachers did not have access to effective professional development and collaboration that occurred tended to be weak and not focused on strengthening teaching and learning. Teachers also reported that much of the professional development available to them was not useful and that they had limited influence in crucial areas of school decision making. In studying teacher perceptions of professional development, Knight (n.d.) reached similar conclusions noting that teachers believed that professional development was impractical, resented top-down decision making in their districts, and experienced anxiety about changes taking place in their schools.

SEVEN CHARACTERISTICS OF EFFECTIVE PROFESSIONAL LEARNING

Enriching educators' professional learning experiences is critical if we are going to realize better outcomes for all students. Seven characteristics of effective professional learning (see Figure 4.1) are outlined in the section that follows.

Effective professional learning takes place over a period of time. It is not a one-shot workshop. Participants are offered opportunities to consider new teaching approaches, test them over time, and determine how they might be improved in practice. Second, effective professional learning reinforces

Figure 4.1 Seven Characteristics of Effective Professional Learning

1. Ongoing
2. Reinforces meaningful collaboration
3. Grounded in educator's practice
4. Involves reflection based on evidence of student outcomes
5. Increases teacher influence
6. Builds capacity for leadership
7. Taps into sources of efficacy

meaningful collaboration—exemplifying the qualities of joint-work. In my experience, teachers' most valuable professional learning results from collaborating with their colleagues. As pointed out by Hargreaves and Fullan (2012), "high-quality peer interaction among professionals doesn't evolve from nowhere or emerge by chance" (p. 87). Change agents must pay attention to both the quantity and quality of collaboration.

Professional learning is also more effective when it is grounded in issues related to student learning that have been identified by participants and when application of new learning is supported onsite. Teachers' everyday work and evidence of student learning outcomes become a rich source for constructive professional learning. Teams of teachers collaborate by posing questions, evaluating their impact, reflecting on their collective work, and determining optimal next steps. As teachers engage in reflective practice, the fourth characteristic of effective professional learning, self-awareness, is enhanced.

Effective professional learning also increases teachers' influence and their power to make decisions on important issues related to school improvement and professional learning. Advanced teacher influence was one of the six enabling conditions for collective teacher efficacy outlined in Chapter 3. Leadership opportunities extend beyond merely serving on a committee or acting as a department or grade-level chair. Structures for teachers to become authentic leaders and decision-makers are provided. Through their leadership and collaborative work, teachers have the potential to become more meaningfully involved in school improvement and catalysts for change.

The seventh characteristic of effective professional learning is that it purposefully and explicitly taps into the sources of collective efficacy (mastery experiences, vicarious experiences, social persuasion, and affective states) and when possible, engages educators in attributional analysis. Building on mastery experiences and providing opportunities for vicarious experiences should be part of an ongoing and deliberate professional learning plan in schools and school districts. In addition, leaders of professional learning need to be aware of and capitalize on social persuasion as well as teachers' emotional reactions to tasks (affective states) as part of a high quality professional learning plan. The importance of teachers' casual appraisals of student performance is outlined in Chapter 1. Teams of teachers often attribute student success and/or failure to external causes. When professional learning is designed to assist teachers in making the link between *their* collective actions and increases in student achievement, it helps in fostering collective efficacy.

When professional learning includes these seven effective characteristics, it is not only more useful to teachers, but it helps also in realizing

Ross and Bruce (2007) designed a professional learning program that explicitly addressed the four sources of efficacy to increase sixth-grade mathematics teachers' efficacy. The researchers attributed the effects of their intervention (increased teacher efficacy) to the elements of the program that were designed to influence sources of teacher efficacy information.

change in schools and classrooms. Long standing beliefs are examined, transfer from theory to practice is more likely, and deeper implementation results. Teachers' perceptions about the value of professional learning change. No longer do they view professional learning as impractical; rather, they see relevant and immediate connections to their classroom practice. As teachers' voices help shape the professional learning, resentment is reduced and anxiety decreases because they have more control over the changes happening in their schools and classrooms. Teachers truly feel empowered.

Models that meet the criteria of effective professional learning are needed. Structures and protocols that reflect the characteristics of effective professional learning are shared in the section that follows. Examples of how the sources of efficacy are fostered through the structures and protocols are shared as well. While a one-size-fits-all approach to enhancing collective efficacy through professional learning does not exist, change agents are encouraged to consider the structures and protocols and determine which to utilize based on their experiences and context.

EFFICACY ENHANCING COLLABORATIVE LEARNING STRUCTURES

Collective efficacy is increased through collaborative learning structures. Leithwood and Jantzi (2008) suggested that efficacy building is closely associated with building collaborative cultures and the structures, which encourage collaboration. Results from a study by Johnson (2012) supported the idea that when teachers work together consistently and frequently, they build each other's capacities. The results also supported that through collaborative work "teachers develop a strong belief that they, as a group can set a course of action and meet their expectations" (p. 100). When structures are in place to support meaningful collaboration, teachers have more opportunities to engage vicariously and gain knowledge about one another's work.

"Deep collaborative experiences that are tied to daily work, spent designing and assessing learning, and built on teacher choice and input can dramatically energize teachers and increase results." (Fullan & Quinn, 2016, p. 63)

Three efficacy enhancing collaborative learning structures are described in the section that follows. Teacher networks, collaborative teacher inquiry, and peer coaching can be utilized to influence staff's interpretations of their effectiveness. These structures provide an organized way to bring people together that helps in moving them beyond established norms to realize greater outcomes for students.

Beauchamp, Klassen, Parsons, Durksen, and Taylor (2014) conducted a study examining the relationship between teachers' professional learning and collective efficacy beliefs over 2 years in five school districts in Alberta. The researchers concluded that collaboration was a powerful theme "accounting for the greatest influence on self-efficacy, collective efficacy, and an important component in all four sources of efficacy" (p. 48). Social persuasion was the highest source of efficacy reported through collaborative activities. Teachers considered social persuasion, such as feedback exchanged within a collaborative partnership, as "a powerful influence on collective efficacy" (p. 48).

Teacher Networks

Collaboration matters; therefore, it would be advantageous to understand the process of change from a perspective that takes into account the dynamics of professional relationships. Change is dependent on relationships within a system. Wheatley (1992) noted that "in organizations, real power and energy are generated through relationships. The patterns of relationships and the capacities to form them are more important than tasks, functions, roles, and positions." As noted earlier, transfer from theory to practice is unlikely to occur via one-shot professional development experiences utilizing outside experts. It is also unlikely to take hold when mandated from the top. Transfer is more likely to happen when teachers build knowledge together. Interdependence of action and connections with other teachers ultimately influence the scale of a proposed change. Therefore, to promote change, it is helpful for leaders to consider how to purposefully connect teachers with one another and draw ties to connect otherwise disconnected individuals and groups.

Connections are made through the formation of teacher networks. Networks are comprised of clusters of schools, or clusters within schools, working interdependently rather than in direct competition. In a network approach, opportunities to meet and connect with educators teaching the same subject, the same division, or who serve

Teacher networks, collaborative teacher inquiry, and peer coaching can be utilized to influence staff's interpretations of their effectiveness.

similar populations of students are frequent. Networks might be configured to connect educators who teach different subjects but share the same group of students (e.g., all teachers teaching students in applied courses in a secondary school), cross panel educators (e.g., Grade 7, 8, and 9 teachers), or educators who share a similar role (e.g., coaches, department heads, administrators). Some networks are formed based on geography (e.g., a high school and its elementary "feeder" schools) or based on involvement in special programs or initiatives (e.g., writing across the curriculum).

Rincon-Gallardo and Fullan (2016) described a network as "a set of people or organizations and the direct and indirect connections that exist among them" (p. 6). Katz, Earl, and Ben Jaafar (2009) described a network as "groups of schools working together in intentional ways to enhance the quality of professional learning and to strengthen capacity for continuous improvement" (p. 9). Sharratt and Planche (2016) described a network as "individuals working together within or across schools to use data to consider a common area of focus as a collective" (p. 71).

The broader purpose of connecting educators is to increase their knowledge about each other's work and increase the spread of high leverage practices. Reeves (2008) suggested that networks provide a viable alternative to hierarchical frameworks for system change arguing that "change throughout a system depends on a distinctly nonlinear communication" (p. 63). Networks provide an opportunity for teachers to learn with and from each other, and therefore, it is a strategy that not only holds potential for enhancing efficacy, but also holds potential for creating and sustaining changes in education.

I witnessed the power of a network a few years ago while working in a school district in Ontario. The district had received a 3-year grant that provided release time for ninth-grade teachers in three secondary schools. The teachers came together to learn about reading and writing strategies that they could use in their content area classrooms. In the first year, the district literacy consultant provided monthly workshops at each separate site and literacy coaches provided follow-up support. An evaluation at the end of the first year revealed that only a few teachers adopted the strategies while the majority failed to see the relevance in their disciplinary subjects. Based on this information, subject-based networks were formed in the second year.

Four times each semester, teachers from each of the three schools, who taught the same subject, were brought together. They identified strategies that *they* felt were relevant to their discipline. For example, upon considering anticipatory strategies, when the literacy consultant introduced the graphic organizer Know-Wonder-Learn (K-W-L), one of the science teachers was reminded of a RAN Chart. Similar to the K-W-L, a RAN graphic organizer has students consider what they know, wonder, and learn, but additional columns allow students to identify what they confirmed (Yes, I was right) and misconceptions (What I couldn't prove). Most of the science teachers were not familiar with the RAN graphic organizer, but all agreed to try it. They valued the RAN over the K-W-L because they saw the relevance in their subject area. From a disciplinary perspective, identifying confirmations and misconceptions was very important to the science teachers. In addition, since they learned about the strategy from a colleague, they were more willing to test it in practice.

As a result of participating in the network, connections with same-subject colleagues were made possible and relationships were built. The configuration of the network afforded educators access to ideas and resources and provided a venue for influential educators to share and therefore spread strategies that worked. Fellow teachers, in turn, tried new strategies, shared what worked for them and what did not, and together, they figured out why. In the second year, most teachers utilized additional release time to further collaborate (the same offer was made in the first year and very few teachers accepted it). Some teachers from the three schools even met on their own time because they saw the value in networking with colleagues teaching the same subject.

In addition to Reeves, a number of leading education experts promoted networks as "a powerful organizational tool" (Katz et al., 2009, p. 3). Katz et al. (2009) outlined a theory of action for networked learning communities for school improvement and suggested that "change will emerge from the *professional knowledge creation and sharing* that occurs through interaction within and across schools in networks" (p. 9). Hargreaves and Fullan (2012) noted that "some of the most powerful, underutilized strategies in all of education involve the deliberate use of teamwork—enabling teachers to learn from each other within and across schools—and building cultures and networks of communication, learning, trust, and collaboration around the team as well" (p. 89). Fullan and Quinn (2016) shared accounts of different networks that were organized to shift practice in organizations across and within districts.

> Reeves (2008) pointed out that change strategies are more likely to be transmitted through a trusted colleague than a superintendent and that "we are more likely to connect to people we have casual contact with than to people separated by hierarchy and distance" (p. 65).

For the purpose of utilizing a network approach as a change strategy to enhance collective efficacy, readers are encouraged to create opportunities that will afford teachers access to ideas and resources. The quality and reach of networks are strengthened over time by connecting effective and influential educators with others and enhancing interactions between sub-groups (e.g., divisions, departments, committees, etc.). In this way, networks strengthen school-based professional learning communities (PLCs). Katz et al. (2009) noted that "networks of schools can both *build from* and *contribute to* within-school PLCs by providing a forum for established and positive organizational learning practices that are situated within school learning communities to be *uploaded* into the network and in turn, *downloaded* to other sites" (p. 17). This is an important element given the fact that "there is more variation in effectiveness among teachers within schools than between schools" (Day, Stobart, Sammons, Kington, & Gu, 2007, as cited in Hargreaves & Fullan, 2012, p. 59).

> Katz et al. (2009) noted that "for networks to be effective, they need to do more than create connections" (p. 8).

City, Elmore, Fiarman, and Teitel (2009) cautioned that some approaches in the network category are not well thought out or well implemented. The authors suggested that "networks need to provide safe spaces for people to learn new approaches, and develop the kinds of cohesion that lets participants support each other—and hold one another accountable—in their instructional improvement work" (p. 62). Rincon-Gallardo and Fullan (2016) also suggested that "when it comes to improving student outcomes across entire education systems, it is not the existence or creation of networks per se that matters but *how they function* and *what they actually do*" (p. 6, emphasis added).

Based on a review of existing research, Rincon-Gallardo and Fullan (2016) identified features of effective networks. Engaging in cycles of collaborative inquiry was one feature identified that speaks to the work performed by networks and how educators within them learn. The authors noted that "collaborative inquiry helps groups stay in a *do* rather than a *talk* mode" (p. 14). Sharratt and Planche (2016) also noted that networked learning communities "whose work only remains at the conversation or research level may simply open the door to more respective relationships between members and reflective conversation" (p. 71). The authors suggested that "adding an important question of inquiry with a commitment to act" (p. 71) helps in changing practice dramatically. Katz et al. (2009) also noted that "collaboration is an important beginning but an insufficient end" (p. 44) when it comes to the activities of a networked learning community and suggested that "collaborative inquiry constitutes the 'work' of effective learning communities in both schools and networks" (p. 46). More about cycles of collaborative inquiry is shared in the section that follows, but first, the relationship between networks and collective efficacy is explored.

Teacher Networks and Collective Efficacy

How is collective efficacy enhanced through teacher networks? In considering the enabling conditions for collective teacher efficacy (see Figure 3.1), knowledge about each other's work is increased through network membership. By breaking down the isolation of the classroom, teachers' feelings of effectiveness and satisfaction are increased as a result of relationships built through networks. In addition, as Reeves (2008) suggested, networks provide a viable alternative to hierarchical frameworks, and thus network structures provide opportunities for advancing teacher influence and responsive leadership.

Kurz and Knight (2003) suggested that the interdependency of teachers contributes to teachers' collective efficacy beliefs. By creating and sharing knowledge while collectively searching for solutions to problems, teachers build confidence in the team's collective capability to handle difficult situations and motivate students. Moolenaar, Sleegers, and Daly (2012) noted that a positive relationship between networks and teachers' perceptions of their collective capability to educate their students is "supported by the idea that teacher interaction offers opportunities to experience the team's ability to promote student learning and to build consensus around shared goals and expectations for students" (p. 253). The authors also noted that when members of a network exchange expertise and provide personal guidance to one another, teachers' beliefs about their collective capacity to solve collective problems, achieve desired goals, and improve school-wide performance increases.

In addition, the work or activities in which the network engages will largely determine the degree to which staff's interpretations of their effectiveness can be influenced. As noted earlier, networked learning community's school improvement work is supported through engagement in collaborative inquiry (Katz et al., 2009; Rincon-Gallardo & Fullan, 2016; Sharratt & Planche, 2016). Additional ways in which collective efficacy is enhanced via collaborative cycles of inquiry are shared in the section that follows.

Moolenaar et al.'s (2012) large-scale research study examined that interplay of teacher collaboration networks, collective efficacy, and student achievement. The researchers found that well-connected teacher networks were associated with strong teacher collective efficacy, which in turn supported student achievement. Most important, the researchers noted that the more *dense* a network—that is, the greater number of existing links or ties in a network in relation to the maximum number of possible ties, the more likely it was for teachers to take risks to improve their school, continuously learn, and try to improve their teaching. Less dense networks were more likely to be involved in the exchange of noncomplex, routine information.

In studying distributed organizations as interdependent networks in relation to the evolution of collective efficacy, Liu, Hu, and Hu (2015) found that organization size, task attributes, and interdependence between subunits had an effect on the collective efficacy. The authors noted that too few or too many group members could reduce a group's efficacy. When tasks were difficult and groups contained few members, teams could not complete the tasks. As group size increased so did the availability of knowledge, experience, and resources. However, more time and effort was needed regarding communication and coordination among members, and diffusion of responsibility was more likely to occur. The researchers suggested that change agents assess task attributes when considering how to determine the size of the team and that offering easy tasks in early stages of group formation will help enhance members' collective efficacy.

Collaborative Teacher Inquiry

Collaborative inquiry provides a systematic approach for educators to identify professional dilemmas and determine resolutions through shared inquiry, problem solving, and reflection. The four-stage model (see Figure 4.2) begins with teachers framing a problem of practice. During this first stage, teachers determine a meaningful focus, develop an inquiry question, and formulate a theory of action. The most effective collaborative inquiry teacher teams keep in mind that their end goal is to increase learning and achieve greater success for *all* students. Therefore, they begin by identifying current student learning needs to ensure that their inquiry is authentic, relevant, and worth the investment.

Teams develop an inquiry question based on the identified student learning needs. When formulating a theory of action, teacher teams compose a sequence of *if-then* statements that illustrate the causality between their actions and expected outcomes. Framing theories in the form of a hypothesis (*if-then*) compels educators to consider *causes* (instructional practices) that precede *effects* (student learning). It helps uncover relationships between teaching and learning as teams examine what they *think* will work against the realities of what is *actually* happening given their existing culture, specific context, and unique population.

Fullan and Quinn (2016) noted that collaborative inquiry is a "promising model used to organize actions for teaching and student learning" (p. 64). Collaborative inquiry is also a promising model that can be used to organize actions for leading and teacher learning.

During Stage 2 of the collaborative inquiry process, teachers work together to develop new knowledge and competencies and implement changes in practice.

Figure 4.2 Collaborative Teacher Inquiry Four-Stage Model

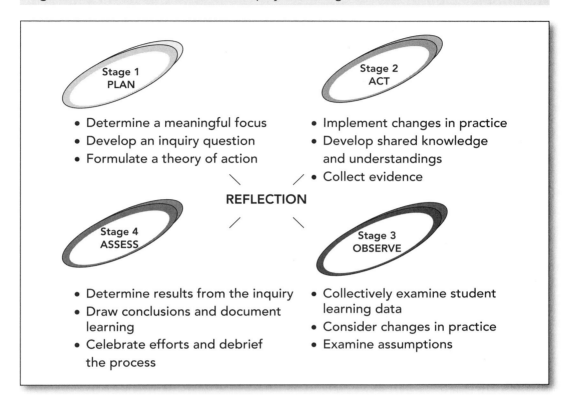

They also identify sources of information that will help answer their inquiry question and collect evidence about how their actions are impacting students. Once teacher teams feel they have gathered enough information to address the inquiry question posed, teams engage in analyzing the evidence (Stage 3). Teachers make meaning of data by identifying patterns and themes and formulating conclusions. As teams refine their thinking, they revisit their theory of action accordingly. During the fourth and final stage, teachers come together to document, share, and celebrate their new understandings. Teams consider next steps by identifying additional student learning needs and reflecting on what they learned through their inquiries. Finally, participants debrief the process by considering how their work was reflective of the characteristics of effective professional learning. Reflection occurs throughout each stage in the cycle.

Katz and Dack (2013) argued that conceptual change is necessary for fundamental school improvement and noted that collaborative inquiry is an "enabler of the kind of professional learning that is about permanent change in thinking or behavior" (p. 7). Changes in beliefs occur as teachers reconcile discrepancies between initial thinking and new ideas that emerge through the examination of evidence and reflection (Donohoo & Velasco, 2016). Furthermore, the qualities of joint-work are exemplified through the collaborative inquiry process. Collaborative inquiry situates teachers' everyday work as the central focus for their learning. Teachers' encounters rest on a shared responsibility for improving student outcomes and interdependence results from the need to draw on each other's experience and expertise to develop more common understandings of student learning needs and instructional practices.

Collaborative Teacher Inquiry and Collective Efficacy

The collaborative inquiry process has been found particularly effective in increasing efficacy. In supporting collaborative inquiry in school districts in both the United States and Canada, I have witnessed the changes in educators' beliefs and practice that result from engaging in cycles of inquiry. Feelings of empowerment often result, and as teachers feel their voices matter. There is also research that demonstrated the positive relationship between collective efficacy and professional learning communities

> Langer and Colton (2005) noted that "schools that engage in collaborative inquiry develop a sense of collective efficacy that helps educators reconnect with their original point of passion: ensuring student success" (p. 26).

characterized by collaboration and inquiry (Voelkel, 2011). Furthermore, Bruce and Flynn (2013) found that teachers engaging in a collaborative inquiry over a 3-year period felt empowered to make instructional decisions together and that the learning design had a "positive impact on teacher beliefs about their abilities to help students learn" (p. 704).

How is collective efficacy enhanced through collaborative teacher inquiry? There are a number of ways. First, the enabling conditions (see Figure 3.1) increased the likelihood that collective efficacy would thrive. The process helps advance teacher influence and increases teachers' knowledge about each other's work. Collaborative school processes also contribute to the cohesion of a staff and support for teachers. Second, the cycle of teacher inquiry provides leaders with an opportunity to enact the leadership practices (see Figure 3.2) that had a high likelihood of

> Tschannen-Moran and Barr (2004) suggested that teacher collaboration might influence efficacy beliefs by creating a climate that legitimizes instructional experimentation, help seeking, and joint problem solving. When educators collaborate and develop solutions to address their problems of practice, efficacy increases.

success of increasing efficacy. The cycle of inquiry provides a structure for meaningful collaboration, empowers teachers, and includes the interpretation of results as a necessary stage in the process. Third, collaborative teacher inquiry is a design that incorporates all seven characteristics of effective professional learning (see Figure 4.1).

Another way in which collective efficacy is enhanced through collaborative teacher inquiry is through analysis of attributions. During a collaborative inquiry cycle, participants' attributions of improved student performance often shift from external causes to teaching as the process requires teachers to examine student outcomes resulting from changes in teaching practices. Gallimore, Ermeling, Saunders, and Goldenberg (2009) provided evidence that the inquiry process helped bring about changes in attributions. Teacher attributions shifted from external causes toward specific, teacher-implemented instructional actions as explanations for achievement gains. Instead of attributing student success and/or failure to factors outside of their control, teachers came to better understand their ability to impact student outcomes. The authors noted that teachers shifted from assumptions that included "I planned and taught the lesson, but they didn't get it" to "You haven't taught it until they've learned" as a result of engaging in a collaborative inquiry process. The researchers believed this shift occurred due to

> *Changes in beliefs occur as participants' attributions of improved student performance shift from external causes to teaching.*

the team's ability to focus on a problem of practice long enough to develop instructional solutions. Seeing causal connections fostered acquisition of key teaching skills and knowledge, such as identifying student needs, formulating instructional plans, and using evidence to refine instruction. In my work supporting collaborative inquiry in school districts, I have witnessed participants' changes in attributions, feelings of empowerment, and increased sense of collective efficacy that accompanies the changes.

Recently, I was invited to a learning fair in a large school district. Teams of educators came together to share the results of their collaborative inquiries and celebrate their learning. As I listened to their stories I heard teams talk about the changes they made to their instructional practice and how these changes had positive impacts on the students in their classes. One team in particular shared that as a result of their inquiry, they could not imagine doing things the way they had in the past. They could never return to their past practice because they collectively witnessed how the changes directly affected their students. The team recognized what they could accomplish together and had already embarked on their next collaborative inquiry.

Preus (2011) contrasted results from groups of new teachers who participated in two different induction programs: a conventional new teacher induction program and one that utilized collaborative teacher inquiry. Teachers taking part in the collaborative inquiry design identified their development as professionals as "grounded in the process of addressing student learning needs" (p. 73) as opposed to teacher needs (as noted by participants in the conventional program). They were more likely to share detailed examples of how and where their learning took place. They defined growth as relating to student achievement as opposed to the wide variety of ways (e.g., progress in time management, organization, and the pursuit of advanced degrees) outlined by participants in the conventional group. Preus (2011) noted that the "strongest examples of learning" were where they were "intertwined with their practice" (p. 75). One conclusion drawn from this study was that "leadership boosts efficacy" (p. 83). The author noted that "given a leadership opportunity, even as a new teacher, there is an immediate urgency to become proficient in the content" (p. 83).

Peer Coaching

Peer coaching is a professional learning structure that employs teachers as partners in developing and trying new strategies and analyzing student learning resulting from classroom instruction. While many coaching relationships assume a hierarchy between the coach and the coachee, peer coaching is not built on this premise. Peer coaching is nonevaluative and based on an environment of trust because teachers are equal partners, serving as critical friends to each other to better understand and improve learning and teaching.

Some types of peer coaching include a preconference and a post conference between the coach and the coachee with an observation in between in which the inviting teacher steers the process (Robbins, 2015). Coaches typically observe aspects of the inviting teachers' practice that have been identified and requested by the inviting teacher. Robbins (2015) pointed out that other types of peer coaching fall under the category of collaborative work and might include study groups, videotaped analysis, and/or a team of teachers co-planning a lesson. In fact, the literature reflects a broad range of activities in which peer coaches might engage.

Given the wide range of activities, for peer coaching to be an effective strategy for fostering collective efficacy, distilling key elements that are related to influencing peer coaches' interpretations of their effectiveness is important. Given the fact that efficacy is increased through vicarious experience—when witnessing someone, facing similar circumstances, meeting with success—observing what happens in the classroom is an important aspect in peer coaching. Void of evidence of student learning, however, it is impossible for teachers to make connections between teaching practices and student outcomes. When observations between peer coaches are focused on teachers' practice alone, opportunities to reflect on casual appraisals and shift attributions are missed. In addition, it is difficult to assess for mastery when observations are focused solely on teacher practice and students are left out of the equation. The peer coaching model described in the section that follows takes these efficacy shaping opportunities into account. The Peer Coaching Cycle (see Figure 4.3) entails four steps: (1) co-planning; (2) teaching (one peer teaches while the other observes, converses, and documents student learning); (3) co-analyzing; and (4) co-reflecting.

Figure 4.3 The Peer Coaching Cycle

Co-Plan
Develop a lesson plan

Co-Reflect
Determine adjustments for
lesson and observations
Reflect on collective efficacy

Peer 1 Teach the lesson
**Peer 2 Observe, Converse,
and Document**
student learning

Alternating Role

Co-Analyze
Analyze student understanding
based on documentation

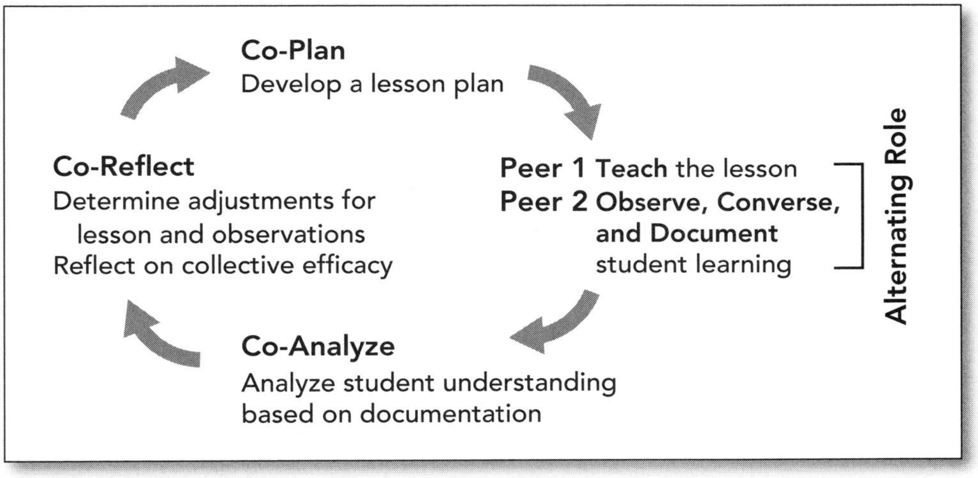

Step 1: Co-Plan

Together, peer coaches share knowledge of successful techniques and explore ideas that might not have been considered before. They bring individual knowledge and expertise as they co-plan a lesson. Co-planning a lesson includes the identification of essential understandings from the curriculum, the articulation of learning intentions in student friendly language, and considerations regarding success criteria. Methods for activating students' prior knowledge, informing students of the learning intentions and success criteria, presenting the content, scaffolding, eliciting performance, and providing students with effective feedback that is targeted at their instructional level are all considered as teachers work together to develop a solid lesson plan.

Step 2: Teach/Observe, Converse, and Document

Next, peer coaches partner in each other's classrooms, alternating classrooms in which the lesson is taught first each time. They also take turns teaching the lesson and observing and conversing with students while documenting student learning. Again, in this model, teachers are not observing each other's practice; rather, they are focused on student learning. The observation process includes engaging in conversations with students in an effort to gain insight into those critical moments when students make connections and develop deeper understandings. Conversations with students about their learning also help uncover gaps between students' current level of attainment and the learning intentions outlined in the lesson.

The documentation of student learning is a critical aspect during this stage in the Peer Coaching Cycle. The homeroom teacher might identify two or three students of interest for the peer coach to focus observations. The peer coach's role in the observation process is to interact with students to delve deeply into student's thinking and document cognitive and metacognitive processes that are being employed by the students of interest. The goal is to help surface strategies and misconceptions so that feedback can be targeted at the students' appropriate instructional level. Peer coaches use a Template for Documenting Student Learning (Resource A) as a means to record observations and conversations.

Step 3: Co-Analyze

During the co-analyzing phase, peers examine the documented student learning. What did they see or hear that suggests that students understand, almost understand, or do not understand? How did the students' responses relate to the lesson taught? What connections did students make? What misconceptions did students have? What does the evidence show that peer coaches did not expect? Do teachers understand students' thinking differently? If so, how? What feedback would help students in closing the gap between current levels of understanding and the learning intentions?

Beauchamp et al. (2014) found that *collaborative peer learning* defined as the preference for peers to serve as coaches was preferred by teachers over having their practice informed by outside experts. Because peers lived and worked "in similar conditions, with similar students, peers help to clarify and affirm ideas in context, and can demonstrate strategies on site, thus serving as role models or learning partners on a more regular, embedded basis" (p. 34).

Step 4: Co-Reflect

The co-reflection phase in the cycle is about determining next steps regarding adjustments to the lesson and documentation of student learning. What worked well? Are there other options for teaching the lesson that teachers might consider? What patterns in students' thinking suggest that the lesson should continue to be taught a certain way, or that it needs modifications or a different approach altogether? If the lesson is taught differently, what are the implications for students? What do teachers need to do to strengthen the collection and documentation of student learning during the Peer Coaching Cycle? What tools can be developed to help capture better evidence of student learning? Do modifications need to be made to templates used to document student learning?

There are also opportunities, especially during this final stage in the Peer Coaching Cycle, for peers to reflect on their perceptions of collective efficacy. As a team, were teachers able to: reach students; motivate students; or find other ways to teach material if students did not understand it the first time?

Peer Coaching and Collective Efficacy

How is collective efficacy enhanced through peer coaching? There are a number of ways. Peer coaching not only reduces isolation, but it also provides a mechanism through which teachers gain deeper insights into student learning while trying new approaches. Peer coaches help each other internalize new practices by supporting the application of teaching strategies in each other's classrooms and engaging in professional discussions about resulting student outcomes. In addition to creating opportunities for meaningful collaboration, peer coaches help each other interpret results and provide each other with feedback, two of the successful leadership practices outlined earlier (see Figure 3.2). Vicarious sources of efficacy are tapped into because teachers observe their peers bringing about student learning. Peer coaches help each other in recognizing success and attributing gains in student learning to classroom instruction. In addition, by providing on-site support and gaining knowledge about each other's practice, collective efficacy is increased through peer coaching.

> Tschannen-Moran and McMaster (2009) found that professional development formats that supported mastery experiences through follow-up coaching had the strongest effect on efficacy beliefs for reading instruction as well as for implementation of the new strategies.

The Student Work Study Teacher (SWST) initiative is a professional learning model in Ontario that supports teacher inquiry into student learning. Much like the peer coaching model described above, the SWST project brought teachers into each other's classrooms to observe students while they were working to figure out what student work was telling educators about how they were doing. The project focused on "capturing and understanding student activity in classroom contexts as the primary source of information used to inform immediate classroom actions and build systematic knowledge of the classroom experience for school, district, and provincial organizational and strategic direction" (Research, Evaluation & Data Management Team of the Literacy and Numeracy Secretariat, 2011, p. 4).

In speaking with one of the SWSTs, she indicated that the key to gaining access into classrooms was that the focus of the observation was student learning rather than teacher practice. Participating teachers felt they had support from the SWST in trying to capture and analyze student learning. Another SWST noted the following, "I have witnessed the power of using student work to drive the decisions that we make in our classroom practice. It was fascinating to watch teacher efficacy improve as students meet success with their learning as a result of their teaching" (Research, Evaluation & Data Management Team of the Literacy and Numeracy Secretariat, 2011, p. 17).

In examining the effects of peer coaching on mathematics teaching practices and teacher beliefs about their capacity to have an impact on student learning, Bruce and Ross (2008) found that peer coaching had a positive impact on teacher efficacy. The authors noted that teacher "judgements about their abilities to influence student learning were affected by the combination of efficacy information sources" (p. 363) and that teachers "received information about their success through peer interaction and observing models of teaching (social and verbal persuasion, vicarious experience, and physiological and emotional cues)" (p. 363).

Collective efficacy resulting from any learning experience is dependent on the effectiveness of the learning structure to address the enabling conditions for collective efficacy and tap into the sources of efficacy. In addition, when the leadership practices that are associated with fostering collective efficacy are ingrained within the learning structures, collective efficacy is more likely realized. Three professional learning structures that meet the criteria for effective professional learning and hold promise for strengthening collective teacher efficacy were shared. In the section that follows, protocols that also support the development of collective efficacy are outlined.

EFFICACY ENHANCING PROTOCOLS

Protocols are guidelines that help focus and deepen conversations. They can be used to help professional learning teams better perform a variety of tasks including examining student work, examining professional practice, identifying and solving dilemmas, and determining key ideas from literature. Some protocols are designed to help teams in developing a shared vision, building trust, gaining consensus, and sharing and celebrating accomplishments. Others are designed to engage participants in deep reflection about the connections between teaching and learning. Six efficacy enhancing protocols are outlined below. Readers will find a short description of each protocol along with rationale regarding how efficacy beliefs are shaped as a result of the protocol. Specific guidelines for each protocol are detailed in the Resources section of this book.

> Fichtman Dana, Thomas, and Boynton (2011) noted that "protocols *systematize* conversation that occurs between educators to *intentionally* focus their dialogue on students and their learning" (p. 13).

Team Success Analysis Protocol

During a Team Success Analysis Protocol (Resource B), teams identify, share, and analyze experiences in which they successfully achieved an outcome that was important to them. When done with an entire faculty, trends are identified and staffs consider how what they learned about achieving success might be applied across the entire school. Since collective efficacy beliefs are shaped through task analysis, including factors that constitute or inhibit success (Goddard, Hoy, & Woolfolk Hoy, 2004), the Team Success Analysis Protocol holds potential for fostering collective efficacy. Teachers' confidence in their peers' competence increases when they hear about each other's successes. In addition, knowledge about one another's work grows through sharing success stories. Finally, collective efficacy is also impacted based on the celebratory nature of the protocol.

> Escobedo (2012) found that teachers who experienced higher numbers of celebrations in schools had "positive views on the effects of the celebrations on their collective efficacy beliefs and the overall competence of the faculty" (p. 83).

Observer as Learner Protocol

The primary purpose of the Observer as Learner Protocol (Resource C) is for the observer to learn how to improve his or her own practice by observing student learning. A secondary purpose of this protocol is to increase efficacy through vicarious experiences. During the observation, the observer makes note of the successes experienced by students. After the observation, the observer reflects on the following: What factors contributed to students' success? What challenges were overcome? How will what I learned today impact my classroom practice? What will I do differently? What do I need to remember to do again? Similar to the Team Success Analysis Protocol, the Observer as Learner Protocol involves analysis of factors that constitute or inhibit success, which contributes to efficacy beliefs (Goddard et al., 2004). By seeing his or her colleague meet with success and identifying factors that contributed to that success, the observer is more willing to try new approaches he or she may have been apprehensive about in the past.

> "Mastery is both an individual and a social construction in which achievements by students are interpreted as evidence of teacher success and failure, thereby contributing to individual and collective teacher efficacy." (Ross, Hogaboam-Gray, & Gray, 2004, p. 166)

Evidence Analysis Protocol

The Evidence Analysis Protocol (Resource D) provides a format for organizing teachers' descriptions and interpretations of evidence of student learning. Teams also collectively determine implications for classroom practice. Teams use student artifacts to track progress and develop deeper understandings of how to support student learning. Examining student work helps strengthen connections between the learning task, content, instruction, and student outcomes. Collaborative analysis helps teachers develop better understandings of how students learn as it "invites multiple interpretations of the same event" (Langer & Colton, 2005). Kazemi and Franke (2004) conducted a study that focused on what teachers learn through the collective examination of student work and noted that "centering the activity on teachers' own student work allowed for conversations that deepened as well as challenged teachers' notions about their work as teachers" (p. 230).

Coming together to share evidence of student learning can sometimes make teachers feel exposed or on the spot, either for themselves or their students. Using a structured protocol to guide the discussion provides an effective technique for maintaining a focus on professional practice, making the distinction between *person* and *practice* explicit. Facilitators of this protocol help team members recognize that teaching can be improved by studying and reflecting on the application of teaching methods and approaches and resulting student outcomes. Criticism is taken less personally when team members come to realize that teaching practices (not individuals) are what is subject to scrutiny.

The process of collectively interpreting evidence of student learning helps individuals understand their own work as they draw on the team's social capital (the collaborative power of the group). When team members contribute ideas and help determine implications for classroom practice, participants not only learn about new approaches, they are more likely to implement them in their own practice. In addition, this protocol helps teachers gain knowledge about each other's work and helps create cohesion among staff. Van Barneveld (2008) found that as a result of using evidence of student learning to drive decision making, teachers reported an increased sense of efficacy.

Diversity Rounds Protocol

Hirsh and Killion (2007) noted that "diversity of opinions, experiences, family background, race, ethnicity, gender, age, location, sexual orientation, disabilities, lifestyle, and socioeconomic status expands our capacity to fully understand reality, to appreciate differences in perspective, and to make decisions that affect student learning that are appropriate, respectful, and informed" (p. 26). The authors also noted that in professional learning the importance of diversity should be recognized because "it enriches the collaborative experience of educators" (p. 25). The purpose of this protocol (Resource E) is to acknowledge the various ways in which a staff is diverse and explore the implications for collective work as it relates to improving student achievement.

Goddard and Skrla (2006) found a statistically significant relationship between collective

Tasan (2000) found that teacher efficacy varied according to the language background of students. Higher teacher efficacy was associated with standard English-speaking students and lower efficacy was associated with non-English speaking students. The researcher also found that diversity training positively influenced teachers' sense of efficacy. This protocol does not constitute a complete program on diversity training, and rather than addressing diversity of students, the diversity of the staff is the focus. It can, however, help a school staff see how their diversity can be capitalized on to better serve their students.

efficacy beliefs and teacher race and experience. Nonminority teachers had a lesser sense of collective efficacy than their minority counterparts. Experienced teachers (more than 10 years' experience) had higher collective efficacy than those with less experience. In addition, faculty ethnic composition explained 46% of the variation among schools in perceived collective efficacy in this study. This protocol can serve as a starting point in helping teachers capitalize on the diversity of the staff to meet the needs of every student in the school. It can serve to initiate socially persuading conversations among diverse subgroups on staff.

Developing a Shared Vision Protocol

Developing a team's capacity to look forward is important in leading effectively, realizing change, and fostering efficacy. Developing a shared vision is about helping teams imagine the way things ought to be. The purpose of engaging in this protocol (Resource F) is for teams to vision a desirable future and describe what is possible. The protocol also assists in helping teams identify the steps, people, actions, and timelines it will take to be successful.

> "The future is not a result of choice among alternative paths offered by the present, but a place that is created—created first in mind and will, created next in activity. The future is not some place we are going to but one we are creating. The paths are not to be found, but made, and the activity of making them changes both the maker and the destination." (Schaar, 1989, p. 321)

Senge (1990) described a shared vision as shared pictures of the future that foster genuine commitment and enrollment rather than compliance to organizational goals and "a force in people's hearts" (p. 206) that provides the focus and energy for learning. By guiding teams in articulating a shared vision, change agents help establish a common sense of purpose and a clear picture of what success looks like among faculty. Senge, Scharmer, Jaworski, and Flowers (2004) noted that "the key is to see the different future not as inevitable, but as one of several genuine possibilities" (p. 25). This protocol helps teams in envisioning how transformations can occur and in realizing that different kinds of futures are possible.

Senge (1990) suggested that creating a shared vision—one that captures the collective mind and will—begins with creative tension. Senge noted that creative tension emerges when we clearly notice where we want to be (the vision) versus where we are now (the current reality). The gap between the two generates creative tension. Similar to how goal setting works (Robinson, Hohepa, & Lloyd, 2009), staff are motivated to take action based on the discrepancy between their current situation and their desired future. A collective sense of efficacy is fostered through teacher empowerment. Shared values are recognized, and

> Kurz and Knight (2003) found that goal consensus on a common vision was the "best predictor of collective teacher efficacy" (p. 122).

as a result staff become more cohesive. They become united based on a common purpose. A cohesive staff was one of the six enabling conditions for fostering collective efficacy.

School Visits Protocol

This protocol (Resource G) provides a means for visitors to a school to engage in meaningful vicarious experiences based on their observations of the school. The protocol helps hosting educators harvest learning from their visitors as well as deepen the learning of the visitors themselves. Teams explore the school, making nonevaluative observations and avoiding qualitative judgments about what is seen. As the team walks around, they discuss what they see, what they wonder about, and what they think the school is working toward.

> Perceptions of efficacy can be modified by sources of information such as observing the performances of others (Bandura, 1997).

IN CONCLUSION

When designing professional learning, it is important to take the dynamics that affect efficacy into account. Collective efficacy is built through shared experiences and vicariously influenced through the observations of successful student outcomes. Assisting staffs in making the link between their collective actions and resulting student outcomes through professional learning will serve change agents well in their quest to foster collective efficacy in schools. As teams engage in reflective practice, self-awareness is increased and direct connections between teaching practice and student learning are made clearer.

Ways to enhance collective efficacy through professional learning were explored in this chapter. Characteristics of effective professional learning were outlined along with professional learning structures and efficacy enhancing protocols. Staffs' interpretation about their effectiveness can be influenced through the establishment of collaborative learning structures. Teacher networks, collaborative teacher inquiry, and peer coaching all have a very high likelihood of fostering efficacy among staff. In addition, protocols can also be used to shape efficacy beliefs. These structures and protocols tap into sources of efficacy, help enable the conditions for collective efficacy to flourish, and assist in shifting attributions from external to internal sources.

In the final chapter, a framework for transferring the research evidence regarding collective teacher efficacy into practice is explored. Readers are guided through a collaborative inquiry process to plan and organize actions, implement changes, observe and monitor outcomes, and reflect on strategies for fostering collective teacher efficacy.

5 Leaders Utilize a Collaborative Inquiry Framework to Organize Actions

Collaborative inquiry is "the methodology for moving a learning focus forward" (Katz & Dack, 2013, p. 39).

Research-based strategies to enhance teachers' perceptions about their ability to collectively impact student outcomes have been shared throughout this book. It is one thing to read about them and another to apply them effectively in practice. In this final chapter, readers are guided through an inquiry process to help bridge the theory-practice divide. A framework for planning and organizing actions, implementing changes, observing and monitoring outcomes, and reflecting on leadership practices is outlined. This framework is designed to assist change agents in using evidence to identify what they need to know, make informed decisions, build capacity, and check on the outcomes resulting from their changed actions over time.

In Chapter 4, collaborative inquiry is introduced as a powerful professional learning design in which *teams of teachers* engage in cycles of inquiry as a means to examine and reflect on teaching practices and resulting student outcomes. Collaborative inquiry is an equally powerful learning design that *leadership teams* can use to examine leadership practices and resulting outcomes. As noted in the opening quote of this chapter, collaborative inquiry is "the methodology for moving a learning focus forward" (Katz & Dack, 2013, p. 39). The premise in this chapter is that the focus for leaders' learning involves figuring out how to transfer the research evidence regarding collective teacher efficacy into practice. The focus for learning is figuring out how to (a) enable the conditions for collective teacher efficacy to flourish, (b) enact the leadership practices that have a high likelihood of success, and (c) put efficacy enhancing professional learning structures and protocols in place. It is not suggested that change agents will take on all this at once. In fact, as a start, readers are encouraged to identify the greatest needs of the staff, focus their learning in one area, put small *moves* in place, and reflect on what was learned as a result.

The methodology, Collaborative Leadership Inquiry Four-Stage Model (see Figure 5.1), is a slightly modified version of the Collaborative Teacher Inquiry Four-Stage Model (see Figure 4.2) presented earlier. Revisions are meant to reflect the fact that just as the practice of teaching can be examined, the practice of leadership can be studied as well. During this first stage, leaders determine a meaningful focus, develop an inquiry question, and formulate a theory of action. During Stage 2, change agents put actions in place and collect evidence that can be used to help inform next steps. Together, leaders develop shared knowledge and competencies as they implement and reflect on changes in practice. The analysis of evidence and examining assumptions occurs during Stage 3, and the final stage involves participants synthesizing new knowledge and identifying what the next iteration of the cycle should entail. Reflection occurs throughout each stage in the process.

> Elmore (2008) noted that "leaders should be doing, and should be seen doing, that which they expect or require others to do" (p. 67). By transparently engaging in cycles of inquiry, leaders not only come to understand, appreciate, and value it as a powerful professional learning design, it also enables them to be better at supporting teachers' engagement in the process.

GETTING STARTED

As the name suggests, the power in the design largely comes from its collaborative nature. Ideally, change agents will not be engaging in the cycle of inquiry alone. If readers are not part of a larger network, whose work is focused on strengthening collective efficacy, they should consider inviting

Figure 5.1 Collaborative Leadership Inquiry Four-Stage Model

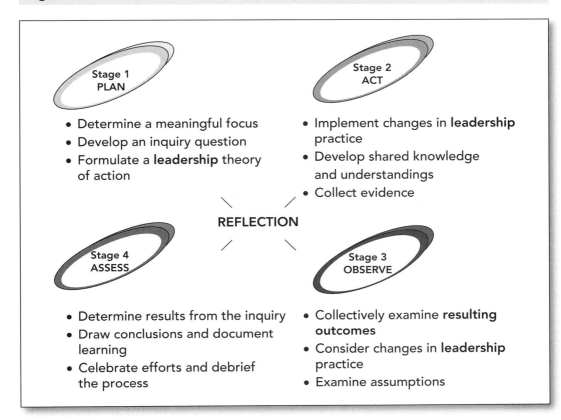

three or four colleagues to take part in an inquiry alongside them. Fichtman Dana, Thomas, and Boynton (2011) outlined three types of inquiry oriented professional learning communities. The first, *shared inquiry*, is characterized by members who define and conduct a single inquiry together. The second, *parallel inquiry*, is one in which the members conduct independent inquiry projects but work collaboratively to support each other's individual endeavors. The third type, *intersecting inquiry*, is characterized by members who engage in individual inquiries that focus on the same topic; however, team members explore different questions or wonderings. Consider which type might work for you and your colleagues as an initial starting point.

STAGE 1: PLAN

Planning involves the framing of a problem. Teams determine a meaningful focus, develop an inquiry question, and formulate a leadership theory of action. In determining a meaningful focus, teams consider current efficacy beliefs, enabling conditions, and contextual factors that might influence efficacy beliefs. For inquiry questions to drive the team's learning, they must come from a place of authenticity. Theories of action are articulated to inform the broader strategy.

Determining a Meaningful Focus

While the problem, for the purposes of this chapter, is framed around strengthening collective teacher efficacy, to gain specificity and determine the greatest need among staff, leaders would benefit from gathering information regarding both current beliefs held by the staff and the extent to which the enabling conditions are in place in their work locations. Also, other contextual factors might be relevant in determining a specific focus for the inquiry during the initial planning stage. These three ideas are expanded upon in the section that follows.

Determining Collective Efficacy Beliefs

Change agents need to be aware of their own and their staff's beliefs if they are going to influence changes in efficacy. There are different ways to determine efficacy beliefs of a staff. Researchers' interest would be in precise measures obtained through psychometrically sound instruments. While the quantitative data obtained from collective efficacy questionnaires provide useful information, day-to-day conversations also provide a rich source of evidence. Rather than administering questionnaires to staffs to determine efficacy beliefs, leaders might simply listen to teachers' everyday conversations to get a sense of what the staff believes. If change agents have belonged to the staff for a period of time, it is likely that they would already have a good sense of the staff's beliefs about their collective ability to impact student outcomes. Researchers' measurement tools and other ideas for determining and capturing collective efficacy beliefs are shared in the section that follows.

Researchers' Measurement Tools. There are different ways in which researchers measure collective efficacy. The most common way is by administering questionnaires that have been designed to measure perceived collective efficacy. Questionnaires usually contain items that ask respondents to indicate their level of agreement using a Likert-style scale ranging from strongly agree to strongly disagree, for example. The following items are examples from Goddard and Hoy's (2003) Collective Efficacy Scale: "Teachers in the school are able to get through to the most difficult students" and "If a child doesn't learn something the first time teachers will try another way." When questionnaires are developed, they are tested for validity and reliability to determine their quality. Goddard and Hoy's (2003) Collective Efficacy Scale and Tschannen-Moran's (n.d.) Collective Teacher Belief Scale are two commonly used valid and reliable instruments. Both are available online and include scoring information.

Typically, researchers administer collective efficacy questionnaires to examine the relationship between collective efficacy and other variables (e.g., students'

When initial interest in measuring collective efficacy began, researchers aggregated scores from self-efficacy questionnaires. Goddard (2001) noted that "aggregation alone is not enough to constitute an organizational characteristic" (p. 468). Bandura (1997) also noted that "perceived collective efficacy is an emergent group-level attribute rather than simply the sum of members' perceived personal efficacies" (p. 478). Therefore, questionnaires were redesigned to reflect the object of the efficacy perception—for example, items measuring collective teacher efficacy are reflective of perceptions based on *we* instead of *I*.

socioeconomic status and/or prior achievement, teacher satisfaction and/or retention, etc.) or prior to an intervention to establish baseline evidence. In the latter case, researchers often re-administer questionnaires at the end of an intervention to determine statistical significance or in other words the degree and direction in which the intervention had an impact.

Change agents will need to determine whether administering a collective teacher efficacy questionnaire is necessary and appropriate based on their specific context and purpose. Since the items on the questionnaires require teachers to share their perceptions of their colleagues' capabilities, the evaluative nature of such responses might raise concerns. Therefore, readers are cautioned to give careful consideration to the purpose of utilizing formal instruments, such as questionnaires, when trying to determine collective efficacy. In cases where formal research regarding collective efficacy is not the intention, other sources of evidence can be used to determine and document change in efficacy beliefs over time. If research is the primary purpose, it is important to adhere to the school district's policies and ethics regarding research.

Paying Attention to Conversations. Conversations present an opportunity to gather evidence of shared beliefs and are perhaps a less intrusive approach than administering a staff questionnaire. The everyday conversations that take place among educators and between educators and students along with the conversations that occur during structured protocols provide a rich source of evidence of collective efficacy and expectancy beliefs. In recalling the site visits with the two secondary school improvement teams, shared at the beginning of Chapter 1, it was the words used by staff members that uncovered collective efficacy beliefs as one staff member noted, "There is nothing that we can do to make a difference with these kids," and another stated, "We have done everything we can at this point."

To determine beliefs, change agents can design and initiate conversations to uncover collective efficacy beliefs. Does the staff believe that they have what it takes to get students to learn or to motivate students? Do teachers feel there is sufficient materials and supplies available to do their job effectively? Do teachers believe they can reach all students? Does the staff feel they have the skills to deal effectively with disciplinary problems? Do teachers feel that community and home issues trump what takes place in schools? Collective efficacy beliefs can be inferred from the conversations that ensue.

A World Café Protocol (Resource H) can be used as an effective way of uncovering efficacy beliefs and capturing conversations. The World Café is a simple and flexible format for hosting a large group conversation. The facilitator provides a prompt and individuals join a group of their choosing and engage in free flowing discussion. There are usually no more than three prompts, revealed one at a time, over a 60-minute session. The conversations are captured in a variety of ways and can be later analyzed for themes. The process can be repeated over time to help determine if changes are occurring. The World Café Protocol is not a structure specifically designed to uncover and capture efficacy beliefs, but given the right prompts it can serve this purpose. For example, prompts might include: Round 1: As a staff, how well can we respond to defiant students and control disruptive behavior? Round 2: As a staff, how much can we do to produce meaningful student learning, help students master complex content, and think critically? Round 3: As a staff, how much can we do to get students to believe they can do well?

> Change agents can model language that focuses on (a) high expectations, (b) growth mindset as opposed to fixed mindset, (c) valuing collaboration as opposed to isolation, (d) attributing results to factors within the team's control, (e) *we* rather than *I*, and (f) the use of social persuasion.

Examining Tasks Assigned to Students. The relationship between expectations and efficacy was described earlier. When teachers have a low sense of efficacy, they hold their students to lower performance expectations. When expectations are low, tasks assigned to students are often low level and lack complexity. Efficacy beliefs could be inferred from the types of tasks teachers are assigning in their classrooms. In addition, change agents could talk to teachers about their performance expectancies to determine efficacy beliefs.

Change agents can work with teams of teachers in examining the level of rigor in tasks using the Assignment Analysis Protocol (Resource I). During the protocol, teams analyze the task and determine the level of thinking required to complete the task. A rigor scale is provided and participants determine what, if any, changes to make to the assignment to increase the level of rigor. Change agents can use this protocol as an opportunity to not only determine collective efficacy beliefs but also to help shape them as well.

Sousa (2013) pointed out the difference between difficulty and complexity and noted that classroom teachers, when designing tasks, often increase the level of difficulty "when it would be much more productive to increase complexity" (p. 9). Sousa distinguished between the two based on the kind of thought involved in each. Difficulty describes how much information is needed to solve a problem. For example, naming the provinces of Canada is a low-level *recall* question. By asking students to name the provinces and their capitals, teachers increase the level of difficulty but the level of complexity remains the same. More complex tasks require analysis, evaluation, and synthesis.

Sousa (2011) also noted that "when teachers are asked whether complexity or difficulty is more closely linked to student ability, they more often choose complexity. Some explain their belief that only students of higher ability can carry out the processes indicated in the *Analyze, Evaluate,* and *Create* levels [of Bloom's taxonomy]. Others say that whenever they have tried to bring slower students up the taxonomy, the lesson got bogged down" (p. 263).

Sousa (2013) cautioned teachers about making assumptions about students who take longer to complete assignments noting that with guidance and practice, students *can* reach the higher levels on Bloom's revised taxonomy.

One final note when considering ways to determine a staff's sense of collective efficacy: People often think that what they believe is the absolute truth. Conversations about collective efficacy beliefs could be perceived as evaluative and threatening to some. If educators feel their beliefs are being questioned or that their beliefs are incompatible with others, negative emotions are likely to surface. Utilizing protocols is one way to minimize

Horton and Martin (2013) noted that when district leaders take a participatory approach to professional learning and develop teachers by sharing leadership and providing for collaborative structures, their involvement can foster trust and aid in the development of a collective efficacy.

threats; however, change agents must also work to develop trust among the faculty. Without trust, teachers will have a more difficult time examining and self-correcting longstanding misconceptions and assumptions underlying their practice (Donohoo & Velasco, 2016). Without the establishment and maintenance of trust as part of the shift in culture, teacher teams may resist engaging in the depth of discussion needed to critically assess their beliefs.

Ways to determine the efficaciousness of a faculty include administering self-report questionnaires, paying attention to conversations, and examining tasks assigned to students. Readers were asked to carefully consider their purpose and heighten awareness of concerns that might be raised when collecting this type of evidence.

Determining Enabling Conditions

When determining a meaningful focus, leaders might also be interested in collecting information about the degree to which the conditions that enable collective efficacy are in place in their schools and school districts. Six enabling conditions for collective teacher efficacy (see Figure 3.1) are shared in Chapter 3. Knowing the extent to which the six conditions exist will help in determining where efforts need to be focused. This information can be tracked over time and used to monitor progress.

The Enabling Conditions for Collective Teacher Efficacy Questionnaire (Resource J) was designed to measure the degree to which the enabling conditions are in place in a school. There are 18 items that provide an overall measure and six subscales that provide a measure for each of the six enabling conditions. Change agents could ask staffs to complete the questionnaire and use the information to determine the priority conditions that need to be addressed to enable collective teacher efficacy. By selecting one or two conditions, leaders can focus their efforts and ensure greater manageability.

Change agents consider staffs' current beliefs about their ability to influence student outcomes and the degree to which the conditions that help foster collective teacher efficacy are in place and use this information to help determine a meaningful focus during the planning stage of the inquiry cycle. Additional contextual factors (e.g., staff turnover) that might contribute to the issue are also important to consider while framing the problem. Therefore, during Stage 1 of the inquiry cycle, as part of the planning process, collaborative inquiry teams are encouraged to obtain information about the staffs' current collective efficacy beliefs, reflect on the degree to which the enabling conditions are in place, and be mindful of what is contextually relevant. Once this information has been gathered, teams can use it to articulate and think more deeply about the problem that is being framed as part of their inquiry.

Developing an Inquiry Question

Once a meaningful focus is specified, collaborative inquiry teams can begin to formulate inquiry questions. When considering how to craft a question, Southern (2015) noted that "a beautiful question is one that challenges assumptions,

> "Crafting and engaging with such beautiful questions is an art. Like other art forms, it takes practice, and requires learning from practice. When practiced well, artful inquiry can lead to transformative learning and innovative change." (Southern, 2015, p. 271)

considers new possibilities, and serves as a catalyst for action and change" (p. 271). Questions posed by collaborative inquiry teams come from a place of genuine curiosity where participants are grappling with issues in which the solution is unknown. "It might stem from a problem of practice that keeps them up at night" (Donohoo & Velasco, 2016, p. 44).

Southern (2015) noted the importance that questions are not prescribed "but rather developed and engaged through a discovery process with those involved in an inquiry" (p. 281). The author also offered the following four considerations for forming great questions. Great questions: (1) generate new thinking rather than quick conclusions, (2) focus on what is desired, (3) generate stories, and (4) are difficult to answer. Teams could use the Inquiry Question Checklist (see Figure 5.2) as a guide to help craft effective inquiry questions.

It is important that teams take the time to craft a rich question as "the power of learning that occurs through the inquiry process can only be as good as the initial questions that frame the entire inquiry journey" (Fichtman Dana et al., 2011, p. 24). In addition, the inquiry question will help drive the data collection, so ensuring the question is authentic, relevant, and thought-provoking is important to the process.

Formulating a Leadership Theory of Action

The final step in the planning stage is to formulate a leadership theory of action. A theory of action "puts into words the steps and contingencies that have to be mastered for a broad vision or strategy to result in concrete action that influences student learning" (City, Elmore, Fiarman, & Teitel,

Figure 5.2 Inquiry Question Checklist

☐ The question generates new thinking rather than quick conclusions.

Look at the situation systemically.

Do not load the question with assumptions about the situation.

☐ The question focuses on what is desired.

Stay away from deficit thinking.

Focus on developing the capacity of the team to work productively with conflict.

☐ The question helps generate stories.

Seek to understand how others think about something.

Encourage context.

☐ The question is difficult to answer.

Create tension.

Benefit from multiple perspectives.

Source: Adapted from Southern, N. (2015). Framing inquiry: The art of engaging great questions. In G. Buche & R. Marshak (Eds.), *Dialogic organization development*. Oakland, CA: Berrett-Koehler.

2009, p. 44). Bushe (2010) described a theory of action map as a map that "consists of our ideas about cause and effect: how to make things happen, how to accomplish tasks and goals" (p. 130). Readers would have encountered my theory of action map about how to help leaders foster collective teacher efficacy (see Figure 3.2). If I am trying to help leaders foster efficacy in their schools and school districts, this map is intended to guide actions, expose the thinking and reasons behind actions, and remove the ambiguity about the change strategy. Bushe (2010) noted that "when we work together to achieve some outcome, our effectiveness depends on our ability to describe, compare, and learn together about our theory of action maps" (p. 132).

Change agents are encouraged to determine key theories of action and talk about them not only with members of their collaborative inquiry team, but also the staff at their schools. As noted earlier, Bushe's (2010) cardwork strategy is one way in which change agents can formulate and articulate their leadership theory of action (see Figure 5.3). A template (Resource K) is provided and outlines the critical components. The title describes what the leadership theory is about, the subtitle articulates the outcomes of successful actions, and the phrases indicate a complete theory of how to reach that outcome. The purpose of the spinning propeller is to

Figure 5.3 Cardwork Strategy: A Leadership Theory of Action

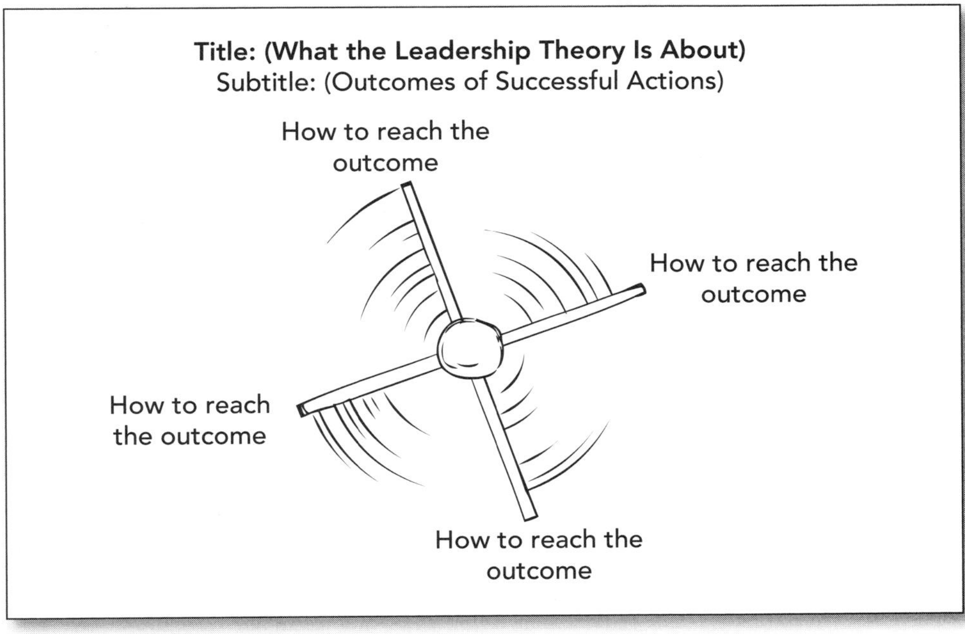

Title: (What the Leadership Theory Is About)
Subtitle: (Outcomes of Successful Actions)

How to reach the outcome

How to reach the outcome

How to reach the outcome

How to reach the outcome

Source: Adapted from Bushe, G. (2010). *Clear leadership: Sustaining real collaboration and partnership at work* (Rev. ed.). Boston, MA: Davis Black. Propeller image courtesy of erich007/iStock/Thinkstock.

show that the critical aspects are not necessarily accomplished in a step-by-step sequence but rather they *spin* to demonstrate a more fluid approach.

I have found creating cardworks very useful in trying to understand my own theories of action as well as those of other people. The map provides a big picture that can be helpful to individuals and teams in identifying smaller moves needed to advance their theory in action. Maps are modified when compared with reality and based on new experiences. "It is in testing the theory through experimentation that the team reshapes their theories based on their experiences and the experiences of their colleagues" (Donohoo & Velasco, 2016, p. 50). As noted earlier, reflection occurs throughout the inquiry cycle. Through reflection, teams discover incongruences between their current theories

> Bushe (2010) suggested that a good basic set of clear maps on topics like success, team work, quality, and dealing with conflict "should be at any manager's fingertips" and encouraged leaders to "experiment with different variations on titles (e.g., success, we succeed, succeeding together), as these can bring up important differences in maps" (p. 161).

and how their theories actually play out in reality. This reflective insight guides further action and interaction, as teams continue to test, revisit, and revise theories accordingly.

STAGE 2: ACT

At this point, the team has collected initial information to help focus their inquiry. The team should have a question that takes into consideration the four suggestions for forming great questions (see Figure 5.2). They have also identified overarching actions they believe will assist them in addressing the problem framed during Stage 1 in the collaborative inquiry cycle. The next stage involves putting actions into practice and increasing leadership capacity by developing knowledge and competencies. Teams

> "Inquiry supports continuous learning and brings people into a space where values, aspirations, and dilemmas can be shared." (Southern, 2015, p. 269)

identify sources of information that will help answer their inquiry question and collect evidence to reflect on the outcomes of their changed actions and determine next steps.

Leaders Implement Changes in Practice

Keeping changes small and frequently reflecting on the changes will help ensure greater success. Heath and Heath (2010) suggested that change facilitators must *shrink the change*, noting that if a task feels too large, people might resist. Teams use their theory of action or cardwork as a tool to determine smaller moves to implement and examine changes in practice. Katz (2015) reported on a project in which supervisory officers engaged in an inquiry process to examine the impact of their school visits in an effort to support administrators as instructional leaders. Supervisory officers engaged in their own inquiries over an 8-month period, using the "plan, act, assess, reflect model to work through incremental 'next best learning moves'" (p. 3). Katz (2015) noted that the "moves were intended to be very small, to allow them to be easy to monitor and learn from" (p. 3). During this stage, change agents identify and test small moves related to their broader theory of action.

Principal Levack's theory of action listed *empowering teachers* as one way to strengthen efficacy. He decided one small move he would take toward empowering teachers would be to seek input in regard to identifying priority issues throughout the school year. By doing so, he believed he was recognizing and honoring teachers' professionalism, establishing a venue for their voices to be heard, and placing decisions related to priority identification in the hands of teachers. His theory was as follows: *If* I ask teachers to identify priority issues for school improvement by asking "What is the most important thing our faculty should focus on to improve the school?" *then* I will learn if the issues I consider as top priorities are the same as the staffs.

The iterative nature of the Collaborative Leadership Inquiry Four-Stage Model involved Mr. Levack reflecting on what he learned through the small move. Mr. Levack learned that priorities identified by teams varied immensely and ranged from issues within their scope of control (e.g., disruptive student behavior) to things that were not within their sphere of influence (e.g., home environment). While engaging in the conversations with staff, he also learned that most of the teachers' perceptions of what they could impact varied from his own ideas. For example, most teachers did not feel students' motivation for learning was something they had much control over. He also learned that a few staff members had no opinion about priority issues, which was something he was not aware of. Mr. Levack used this information to determine his next small move.

Teams Develop Shared Knowledge and Understandings

Building individual and collective knowledge is inherent in the inquiry process as the design is rooted in constructivist theory. Change leaders generate knowledge and meaning as they move through the stages, co-constructing new understandings through *learning by doing*, and reflecting on the impact of the moves articulated in their theories of action. It would serve teams well to identify resources that would be useful in gaining deeper understandings about how to foster collective teacher efficacy. Locate and share primary and secondary sources. Talk with each other about the latest research. (*Note:* The reference list at the end of this book would be a great starting point.) Teams could identify and reach out to external experts as well as learn more about collective teacher efficacy and how to hone their leadership practice in an effort to foster it. Understandings about both collective efficacy and leadership practice are deepened as a result of authentic engagement in the inquiry cycle.

Collecting Evidence

As noted earlier, based on the iterative nature of the inquiry cycle, reflection is frequent and based on evidence collected. Individuals collect and examine evidence to inform their next small move as well as their broader strategy. Katz (2015) posed three questions to help focus the collection of evidence. The questions included: (1) What will success for this move look like?; (2) What do I hope to learn from this move?; and (3) What conversations, observations, and/or product will I look at to evaluate the success of my learning move? Teams would benefit from considering these three questions at this stage in the cycle.

Teams test their theories of action by identifying small moves and enacting the theory in practice. They develop shared knowledge and understandings by engaging outside experts, reading and talking about relevant research and articles, and putting moves into place and reflecting on their leadership practice. Teams consider evidence in light of the small moves identified based on the broader theory of action. In considering evidence, teams identify what success looks like, what they hope to learn from the small move, and what they can look at to evaluate the success of their small moves. During Stage 3, teams will revisit various components from Stages 1 and 2 as they continue to learn and hone their skills and approaches. For example, as teams learn more about ways to enhance efficacy and consider what evidence to collect, it is likely that they will revise their inquiry question. This is a natural part of the process.

STAGE 3: OBSERVE

Observing requires an open, nonjudgmental attitude and setting aside any preconceived notions about what you think ought to be. It is about being interested in learning more about yourself and others and requires the examination and suspension of assumptions. It also requires a certain amount of objectivity. During this stage in the cycle, teams benefit from considering outcomes that resulted from their small moves. When evidence is shared and collectively interpreted, different perspectives help shed light on the results from changes in practice.

Teams Collectively Examine Resulting Outcomes and Consider Changes in Leadership Practice

Collecting evidence at this phase is notably different from what was described during the planning stage. Readers will recall that when determining a meaningful focus, ways to measure collective efficacy beliefs and tools for measuring the extent to which the enabling conditions were in place were shared. While this information was important to establishing baseline data, evidence collected and examined during the act (reflect) and observe (reflect) stages of the cycle is focused on outcomes from the small moves so that adjustments in leadership actions can be made based on reflection and in an effort to hone practices so that they are the most impactful. Therefore, the frequency in which the evidence is collected, examined, and reflected on during the act and observe stages allows participants to cycle back and forth between these two stages. Teams cycle back and forth between acting and observing as they develop deeper understandings about their problems of practice and gain insights about how leadership could be cultivated through their actions and interactions with others.

Katz (2015) posed the following questions that are useful to consider at this stage in the cycle: "What happened? What did I find out? What did I learn from this move? What did I learn about this move as a transferable leadership practice?" (p. 4). Katz noted that what participants learn *from* the move provided information pertinent to the specific challenge of practice "and how to move forward with it" (p. 8), whereas what was learned *about* the move provided information on "whether the move itself was a good one and worth replicating" (p. 8), labelling what is being learned about leadership.

Also, the importance of individual contributions to the team is highlighted in Katz's (2015) supervisory officer study. Findings included that "the power of a learning network is in each person working on his/her own slice of the problem, with the network aggregating the learning" (p. 6) and that by hearing about others' inquiries, the team considered new ideas both for themselves and for their school districts.

Examining Assumptions

While participants cycle between the stages of acting and observing, it is important to revisit their theory of action. How has the theory of action played out? In light of the team's interpretation of evidence, the team considers what holds true in their theory of action and what might require a revision. Sparks (2007) referred to a *theory of action* as "a set of underlying assumptions about how the organization will move forward from its current state to its desired future" (p. 38). The author also cautioned that "these assumptions affect improvement efforts whether they are hidden from us because we never consciously considered them or are explicit because we have thoughtfully reflected upon their efficacy and articulated them to others" (p. 38). Teams benefit by uncovering the assumptions in their theories and reflecting on them as a group.

In summary, Stage 3 involves objective observation of outcomes that resulted from changes in leadership practices. Change agents determine small moves based on a broader theory of action and consider what they learned *from* and *about* the move (Katz, 2015). Together, individuals learn more about ways to strengthen collective efficacy by acting and observing and reflecting on the leadership practices. The next stage in the cycle involves determining results from the inquiry, drawing conclusions, and debriefing the process.

STAGE 4: ASSESS

Assessment at this stage involves asking the following questions: What did we learn about our practice of leadership? What is the answer to our inquiry question(s)? What conclusions can we draw based on the evidence? Has collective efficacy increased? Have the conditions that enable efficacy to flourish improved? Teams determine the results from their inquiry, document their learning, and celebrate efforts.

Teams Determine Results From the Inquiry

While teams examined evidence from the smaller moves during Stage 3 (observe) in the inquiry cycle, Stage 4 (assess) involves assessment of the broader plan. To answer the questions posed in the above paragraph, teams could revisit the diagnostic tools used during the planning stage. Depending on how much time has passed, the team might consider recollecting information about efficacy beliefs and/or the extent to which the enabling conditions are in place to determine if changes have occurred.

Drawing Conclusions and Documenting Learning

One of the final steps in the inquiry process is drawing conclusions. Teams determine the implications of their findings and articulate an answer to their initial inquiry question(s). This step is about attaching meaning and significance and determining what is really important. In addition, recommendations and next steps are identified. Teams decide on a format for documenting and sharing their findings with a wider audience. "Documenting the work not only concludes the collaborative inquiry cycle, it also encourages further reflection and helps consolidate understanding" (Donohoo, 2013, p. 82). Documentation is not meant to be an onerous process. Teams only need to determine the best way to share their learning so that others can benefit from the knowledge generated by the team.

Celebrating Efforts and Debriefing the Process

In this final stage, it is important to celebrate learning and debrief the process. This is an important final step as debriefing will not only bring closure to the process; it also will help further develop the team and provide direction for the future. It also helps the leadership team in recognizing how the inquiry process can be a useful way to tackle adaptive challenges and build leadership capacity. Characteristics of Collaborative Leadership Inquiry Continuum (Resource L) has been included as a tool that teams can use to debrief the process. It includes statements related to the five characteristics that play a critical role in helping collaborative inquiry team members build adaptive capacity (Donohoo, 2013). Characteristics include: (1) the process is collaborative, (2) the process is reflective, (3) engagement requires that participants take a learning stance, (4) the process is driven by practice, and (5) actions are informed by evidence. The original Characteristics of Collaborative Inquiry Continuum (Donohoo, 2013) was modified and reframed from a perspective that takes leadership practice as opposed to teaching practice into account. Change agents who took part in the collaborative leadership inquiry consider the team as a whole and determine where along the continuum they would place the team concerning each statement. Team members come together to discuss strengths and areas for improvement.

Finally, by acknowledging the effort of the team and celebrating the professional learning that occurred through the collaborative inquiry process, change agents will feel respected. Celebrations signal what is important and reinforce shared values (DuFour, 1998). Another reason to celebrate is to make evident the accomplishments that resulted from teamwork. Celebrations help highlight the power of working together as a team, which sets a great example for teacher teams while contributing to the development of the collective efficacy of change leaders.

IN CONCLUSION

The Collaborative Leadership Inquiry Four-Stage Model described in this chapter along with the tools provided will assist change leaders in measuring the collective efficacy beliefs of the staff, determining the degree to which the enabling conditions are in place within their schools, implementing changes in leadership practice, monitoring results, and determining next steps. In addition, by engaging in a cycle of inquiry, leaders are modelling best practices for their staff. They are seen doing what they expect others to do. Having experienced it themselves, leaders are better able to guide teachers through the process. Leaders come to understand, appreciate, and value collaborative inquiry as a powerful professional learning structure.

As noted throughout this book, fostering collective teacher efficacy is a timely and critical issue if we are going to realize student success. The power of efficacy beliefs was highlighted and change agents were called to action to focus school improvement efforts on cultivating collective efficacy. While a large portion of this book translated the research on collective efficacy into a form that is accessible to educators, a number of practical strategies and tools were shared. Six enabling conditions were detailed along with a tool to measure the degree to which the conditions are in place in schools (Resource J). Four leadership practices that have a high likelihood of strengthening collective efficacy were outlined. Readers were encouraged to implement the professional learning structures and protocols to enhance collective efficacy and utilize a collaborative inquiry design to organize leadership actions.

Bennett (2011) noted "from my take on what I've seen over the years, we seem to enjoy researching, writing and attending workshops on change more than we do enacting change meaningfully over time" (p. 14). By engaging in the Collaborative Leadership Inquiry Four-Stage Model, change agents put into practice what was gleaned from the research on strengthening collective efficacy. The model provides a structure to not only enact change but also to determine the effectiveness of the changes and make the necessary adjustments to realize increases in collective efficacy.

One final note: Change takes time. Changing the fundamental beliefs held by educators is not an easy endeavor. Helping educators understand how their efficacy beliefs come to fruition through their actions will increase self-awareness and the likelihood that educators will be more reflective about their practice. Encourage constant reflection, call on the power of the collective, and stay the course. Given its effect on student achievement, the importance of strengthening collective efficacy must not be understated or overlooked.

RESOURCE A. TEMPLATE FOR DOCUMENTING STUDENT LEARNING

LEARNING GOALS	SUCCESS CRITERIA

Demonstrations of Learning	Misconceptions
Cognitive Strategies Used by Students	**Metacognitive Strategies Used by Students**

RESOURCE B. TEAM SUCCESS ANALYSIS PROTOCOL

During this protocol, it is important to help the school staffs stay focused on how the successes, described by each team, were different from more routine work. The analysis of what led to success and identifying trends across teams are the purposes of the protocol.

There is an assumption that teams have been established and working together, over time, to achieve a common outcome.

> *Success* is defined as something that proved to be highly effective in achieving an outcome important to each team.

Total Time: 1 hour

Step 1 (5 minutes)

Group Configuration: School Teams

Together, teams identify and write a short description of a success they have experienced in terms of their work (with students, using a common teaching strategy, peer coaching, engaging in cycles of inquiry, etc.).

Guiding Questions

- What are the specifics of the success?
- What made the experience different from others like it?
- What did it mean in terms of your team's work (as teachers, administrators, coaches, with students, with your colleagues, using a common teaching strategy, peer coaching, etc.)?

Step 2 (25 minutes)

Group Configuration: Mixed—representatives from different school teams

In groups of four to five, participants take turns describing their team's successful experiences in as much detail as possible. As each presenter shares his or her team's story, the others take notes and are provided an opportunity to ask clarifying questions. During this round, each participant is provided the opportunity to reflect upon the successes shared. The purpose of this step is to uncover why teams were so successful—to see more in the successes.

Guiding Questions

- Why did your team think . . . ?
- What was different about . . . ?
- Why did your team decide to . . . ?

Step 3 (10 minutes)

Group Configuration: Same as above

The group reflects on the success stories and discusses what they heard each presenter say and offer additional insights and analysis of the successes. The group of four to five identifies and lists the factors that contributed to each team's successes. The group then discusses briefly how what they have learned might be applied to the work of the entire staff.

Step 4 (10 minutes)

Group Configuration: Faculty/School Staff

Each group of four to five shares their list of factors that contributed to each team's successes with the larger group (entire faculty). The large group looks for trends across groups and then discusses what it would mean to consciously create conditions that lead to successes.

Step 5 (5 minutes)

Group Configuration: School Teams

Teams come back together to celebrate their success and briefly discuss next steps based on the discussion from Step 4.

Step 6 (5 minutes)

Group Configuration: Faculty/School Staff

The staff debriefs the protocol.

Guiding Questions

- What worked well?
- What misconceptions or confusions emerged?
- What adaptations to this protocol might improve the process?
- How might we apply what we learned to other work?
- How might others (teachers, administrators, students) use this process to reflect on their work?

Source: Adapted from the National School Reform Faculty. (n.d.).
Retrieved from http://www.nsrfharmony.org/system/files/protocols/success_analysis_reflective_0.pdf

RESOURCE C. OBSERVER AS LEARNER PROTOCOL

During this protocol, an observer is invited into a peer's classroom to observe student learning. The observer's primary purpose is to learn how to improve his or her own practice by observing students. A secondary purpose of this protocol is to increase efficacy through vicarious experiences.

Note: This protocol might be used by peer coaches in conjunction with a Template for Documenting Student Learning (Resource A) as part of the Peer Coaching Cycle. If peer coaching is not established, this protocol would stand on its own. If peer coaching is an established practice, this protocol might be considered during the Observe-Converse-Document stage in the Peer Coaching Cycle (see Figure 4.3) and the purpose of improving practice would be extended to both parties involved.

> Up to two to three teachers might observe students in a colleague's classroom at the same time.

Step 1: Orientation

If the lesson that is going to be taught was not co-planned, a preconference would help to orient the observer as to what will be happening. What are the learning goals for the lesson? What was previously taught? How much time will the lesson take? The observer determines if he or she wants to focus on all students, a small group of students, or one to two students of interest.

Step 2: Observation

The observer watches the lesson taught and listens to and interacts with students as they engage in learning. The observer makes note of the successes experienced by students.

Step 3: Reflection

The observer reflects on the following questions:

- What factors contributed to students' success?
- What challenges were overcome?

- How will what I learned today impact my classroom practice?
- What will I do differently?
- What do I need to remember to do again?

Source: Adapted from the National School Reform Faculty. (n.d.).
Retrieved from http://www.nsrfharmony.org/system/files/protocols/observer_as_learner.pdf

RESOURCE D. EVIDENCE ANALYSIS PROTOCOL

The Evidence Analysis Protocol provides a format for organizing teachers' conversations by clearly defining who should be talking when and about what. While at first it may seem rigid and artificial, a clearly defined structure frees the team to focus its attention on what is most important—evidence of student learning. The facilitator's aim is to shift conversations from generalized talk about student's progress and polite sharing of teaching strategies to more in-depth conversations about the connections between the two.

> The term *evidence*, rather than *data*, is used throughout this protocol. The term *data* is often associated with numbers. When using the broader term *evidence*, school improvement teams are encouraged to consider both qualitative and quantitative information.

Selecting Evidence to Share

Student learning evidence is the centerpiece of the team's discussion. The following guidelines can help in selecting artifacts that will promote the most interesting and productive team discussions. Evidence of student learning includes the day-to-day assessments and evaluations teachers make about student learning. Sources include student work products, observations, and conversations. Standardized tests also provide a rich source of student learning data. Presenters might select one or a few students of interest to help manage the process.

Total Time: 50 minutes

Step 1: Getting Started (5 minutes)

The educator sharing the student learning evidence gives a very brief statement of the work and avoids explaining what he or she concludes about it.

Step 2: Describing the Evidence (10 minutes)

The facilitator asks: What do you see?

During this period the team gathers as much information as possible from the evidence. Team members describe what they see in student learning evidence, avoiding judgments about quality or interpretations.

Note: If judgments or interpretations do arise, the facilitator should ask the person to describe the evidence on which they are based. It may be useful to list the team's observations on chart paper. If interpretations come up, they can be listed in another column for later discussion during the interpretation phase.

Step 3: Interpreting the Evidence (10 minutes)

The facilitator asks: What does the evidence suggest?
Follow-up questions might include:

- What do you see or hear that suggests students understand, almost understand, or do not understand?
- Which students are understanding, almost understanding, or not understanding?
- What does that tell us?
- What do you see or hear that you did not expect to find?
- What are the assumptions we make about students and their learning?

During this period, the group tries to make sense of what the evidence says and why.

The team should try to find as many different interpretations as possible and evaluate them against the kind and quality of evidence.

Step 4: Implications for Classroom Practice (10 minutes)

The facilitator asks: What are the implications of this work for classroom practice?

This question may be modified, depending on the evidence.

Based on the group's observations and interpretations, discuss any implications this work might have for teaching and assessment in the classroom.

Follow-up questions might include:

- What steps could be taken next?
- What strategies might be most effective?
- What else would you like to see happen?
- What kinds of assignments or assessments could provide this information?
- What does this conversation make you think about regarding your own practice?

- About teaching and learning in general?
- What are the implications for equity?

Step 5: Reflecting on the Evidence Analysis Protocol (10 minutes)

Presenter Reflection:

- What did you learn from listening to your colleagues that was interesting or surprising?
- What new perspectives did the team provide?
- How can you make use of your colleagues' perspectives?

Group Reflection:

- What questions about teaching and assessment did looking at the evidence raise for you?
- Did questions of equity arise?
- How can you pursue these questions further?
- Are there things you would like to try in your classroom as a result of looking at this evidence?

Step 6: Debrief the Process (5 minutes)

The facilitator asks:

- How well did the process work?
- What about the process helped you see and learn interesting or surprising things?
- What could be improved?

Source: Adapted from the National School Reform Faculty. (n.d.).
Retrieved from http://www.nsrfharmony.org/system/files/protocols/atlas_looking_data_0.pdf

RESOURCE E. DIVERSITY ROUNDS PROTOCOL

The purpose of this protocol is to acknowledge the various ways in which a staff is diverse and explore the implications for collective work as it relates to improving student achievement.

Total Time: 40–60 minutes
(depending on the number of rounds)

Step 1: Introduction (5 minutes)

The purpose of the protocol is shared. Participants are informed that the facilitator will call out categories for subgroups to form. The facilitator indicates that the subgroup categories will be *vague* and that it is up to individuals to define for themselves which subgroup they will go to.

Step 2: Forming Subgroups (10 minutes)

The facilitator chooses categories, generally going from lesser to greater levels of sensitivity. Categories should fit the staff's purpose. Once the subgroup has formed, they have a brief discussion about the impact of this particular identity on their collective work.

Examples: Where you are from; the kind of high school you went to; birth order; your hobbies; the kind of student of mathematics you were; area of study for your undergrad; your teachable subjects; your gender; your ethnicity.

Step 3: Reporting (5 minutes)

After members of each subgroup have talked among themselves, they report out.

Step 4: Regrouping (10 minutes or more, depending on the number of rounds)

The facilitator announces a new category. Groups reform and have the same discussion about impact of this new identifier. Facilitators determine how many rounds to call for subgroups.

Step 5: Debriefing (10 minutes)

Participants discuss feelings that emerged during the activity, along with any insights about the meaning and impact of diversity and its effects on professional experience. What are the implications for their collective work as it relates to meeting the needs of each and every student? How can the staff build on individual strengths and diversity to accomplish their collective goals?

Source: Adapted from National School Reform Faculty. (n.d.).
Retrieved from http://www.nsrfharmony.org/system/files/protocols/diversity_rounds_0.pdf

RESOURCE F. DEVELOPING A SHARED VISION PROTOCOL

The future is not a result of choice among alternative paths offered by the present, but a place that is created—created first in mind and will, created next in activity. The future is not some place we are going to but one we are creating. The paths are not to be found, but made, and the activity of making them changes both the maker and the destination. (Schaar, 1989, p. 321)

One purpose of this protocol is to vision into the future and tell what it would look like in the very best-case scenario. Another is to initiate discussion into the steps, players, actions, and timelines it will take to be successful.

Goals

- To expand and clarify the vision of what a team is really trying to accomplish
- To identify opportunities and avenues for focused improvement
- To guide purposeful actions and reduce wasted efforts

Presentation is made by members of a team who have similar investments in and context to that which is presented. The team should not focus on obstacles, but rather the opportunities, and stay positive throughout.

Total Time: 45 minutes

Step 1: The Team Presents What It Is They Are Trying to Accomplish (5 minutes)

The team shares what they are trying to do and how it might look when it is all done.

Step 2: Probing Questions (10 minutes)

The team raises probing questions to the whole group with perhaps no real expectation of answering them in this step. The idea is to extend the thinking about what they want to accomplish.

Step 3: Project Into the Future (10 minutes)

The team considers a timeline that would seem appropriate and thoroughly describes what it looks like, sounds like, and feels like having accomplished this endeavor.

Tips: Talk in present tense and describe the best-case scenario. The team does not yet describe how. Focus on the sights, sounds, behaviors, and feelings surrounding this accomplishment.
    For example:

- 5 years later in a school's reform efforts
- The end of a team's project with students

Step 4: Look Back (10 minutes)

The team looks back to describes how things were when the project started.
    Discuss how the team addressed the starting place and how they moved from that to the projected present.

Tips: Talk in past tense. Think about issues, culture, conversations, teacher's work, student achievement, and so on. Try to remain as tangible as possible. Teams might chart this conversation. It is helpful to put dates at the top of the chart to identify the time period to which the group is referring. Directly relate the previous description of how it looked when it started. Consider discussing how, when, with what resources, and by whom.

Step 5: Return to Projected Future (5 minutes)

Discussion revolves around whether the project can get any better than it is or whether this is as good as it could possibly be. Again, the team thinks about how it will look, sound, and feel if it can get even better.

Step 6: Debrief the Process (5 minutes)

The facilitator asks:

- How did this protocol work for you?
- What might you do differently next time?

Source: Adapted from the National School Reform Faculty. (n.d.).
Retrieved from http://www.nsrfharmony.org/system/files/protocols/future.pdf

RESOURCE G. SCHOOL VISITS PROTOCOL

This protocol provides a means for visitors to a school to have a meaningful interchange with hosting educators about their observations of the school. This protocol can help hosting educators harvest learning from their visitors and deepen the learning of the visitors themselves. The protocol can be used while school is in session or after school hours.

Total Time: 60 minutes

Step 1: School Walk (20 minutes)

Pair up in cross-school pairs and walk through the host school.

Make nonevaluative observations, avoiding qualitative judgments about what is seen.

As your team walks around, discuss the following questions:

- What do you see?
- What don't you see?
- What do you wonder about?
- What do you think this school is working on?

If you are a member of the school's faculty, don't give a tour, explain, apologize, or show off. Look at your school and participate in the protocol with a beginner's mind.

Step 2: Sharing Observations (20 minutes)

Return to the large group and share your findings on the questions in sequence.

Step 3: Host Reflections (10 minutes)

People in the group who work in the school reflect aloud on what they heard that surprised and interested them and what they saw during their walk that was new.

Step 3: Implications for Education (5 minutes)

Discuss the implications of the observations for education.

Step 4: Debriefing the Protocol (5 minutes)

Debrief the protocol. Was it valuable? How could it have been better? How might this protocol be put to use in the future?

Source: Adapted from the National School Reform Faculty. (n.d.).
Retrieved from http://www.nsrfharmony.org/system/files/protocols/school_walk_0.pdf

RESOURCE H. WORLD CAFÉ PROTOCOL

The World Café Protocol provides a simple, effective, and flexible format for large group conversations.

Total Time: 60 minutes (5 minutes for introduction and 18–20 minutes per round)

The environment (modeled after a café) should include small round tables with four to six chairs at each table. Large chart paper and markers should be available at each table.

Step 1: Welcome and Introductions (5 minutes)

The facilitator begins with a warm welcome and an introduction to the World Café process, setting the context, sharing the Café etiquette, and putting participants at ease.

Participants are informed that there will be three rounds of discussion, prompted each time by a question(s). People are encouraged to consider the question, listen to other's perspectives, and share their own. Participants are encouraged to capture the conversation on the chart paper using words, images, or symbols. They are encouraged to connect ideas and using probing questions to fully understand each other's ideas and/or contributions. Each table group is asked to nominate (or have someone volunteer) to host the conversation. The table host will remain at the same table for all three rounds and it's his or her responsibility to welcome new people (for each new round) and summarize previous conversation (referring to what was captured on the chart paper).

Step 2: Round 1 (18–20 minutes)

The process begins with the first of three rounds of conversation for the small group seated around a table. The facilitator shares the first of three questions and sets a timer for 18 to 20 minutes.

Step 3: Move to Round 2

At the end of the 20 minutes, each member of the group moves to a new table of his or her choice. The group does not move as a whole. The host remains at the table, welcomes new participants, and briefly shares what was discussed during the first round.

Step 4: Round 2 (18–20 minutes)

The facilitator shares the second of three questions and sets a timer for 18 to 20 minutes. Participants are encouraged to record their thoughts, ideas, and suggestions on the chart paper.

Step 5: Move to Round 3

At the end of the 20 minutes, each member of the group moves to a new table of his or her choice. Again, the host remains at the table, welcomes new participants, and briefly shares what was discussed during the second round.

Step 6: Round 3 (18–20 minutes)

The facilitator shares the final question and sets a timer for 18 to 20 minutes. Participants are encouraged to record their thoughts, ideas, and suggestions on the chart paper.

Step 7: Harvest

After the small groups (and/or in between rounds, as needed), individuals are invited to share insights or other results from their conversations with the rest of the large group. These results are reflected visually in a variety of ways, most often using the chart paper in the front of the room.

Source: Adapted from http://www.theworldcafe.com/key-concepts-resources/world-cafe-method

RESOURCE I. ASSIGNMENT ANALYSIS PROTOCOL

Purpose

This protocol is particularly useful when a team is learning to:

- effectively plan, create, and assess the outcomes of powerful lessons; and
- increase the rigor of instructional and assessment practices.

Preparation

Select an assignment to be analyzed for its effectiveness. Keep in mind that the assignment may be under scrutiny. Depending on the level of comfort that is established within the group, it may be helpful to begin this process with an assignment that was not developed by any individual member of the team.

Process

Step 1: Examine Curriculum Expectations

- Post and collaboratively review the identified expectations from the curriculum that are being targeted through the current instruction.
- Brainstorm the likely success criteria for the various expectations.

Step 2: Analyze the Task

- Take a couple of minutes to read and reflect on the task that is up for discussion.
- Collaboratively create a chart or organizer first, jotting down which expectations are targeted through the assignment, then link the related success criteria to the evidence that will be used to determine if students have learned the desired outcomes.
- On the basis of your own experience, break down the task. List what students have to know and be able to do to complete the task successfully. Be as specific as possible.
- Engage in working on the task while noting the knowledge, skills, and abilities required to successfully complete the task.
- Determine the level of thinking required. What are the levels of Bloom's Taxonomy that apply to this assignment? Justify your selection(s).
- Assess for desired level of rigor. Using the rigor scale, determine whether the task is appropriately rigorous.

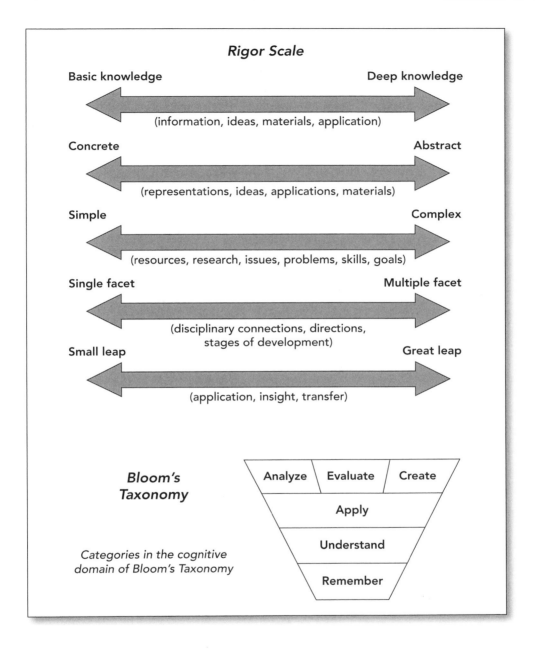

Step 3: Analyze the Lesson

- Discuss the following questions:
  - How did the teaching prepare students for this task?
  - What scaffolds were provided?

○ What could be added to the instruction to better prepare students to successfully demonstrate their knowledge, skills, and/or abilities?

○ Does the instruction provide students with the opportunity to demonstrate what they know and can do based on the curriculum expectations?

Step 4: Revise the Assignment Accordingly

Revise the assignment, prompt, or task according to your work in Steps 1–3.

Step 5: Debrief the Process

What did your team discover? How did the process work for the team?

Source: Adapted from Learning Forward Ontario. (2014). The power of protocols. Retrieved from http://learningforwardontario.ca/files/Power_of_Protocols.pdf

RESOURCE J. THE ENABLING CONDITIONS FOR COLLECTIVE TEACHER EFFICACY QUESTIONNAIRE

Directions: Please indicate your level of agreement with each of the following statements about your school from **strongly disagree** to **strongly agree**. Your answers are confidential.

1 = Strong Disagree   2 = Disagree   3 = Somewhat Disagree
4 = Somewhat Agree   5 = Agree   6 = Strongly Agree

1. Teachers are entrusted to make important decisions on school-wide issues.   1 2 3 4 5 6

2. Improvement goals are established and understood by all faculty.   1 2 3 4 5 6

3. Administrators help us carry out our duties effectively.   1 2 3 4 5 6

4. The staff holds shared beliefs about effective instructional approaches.   1 2 3 4 5 6

5. Teachers are provided authentic leadership opportunities.   1 2 3 4 5 6

6. I know about the classroom management strategies my colleagues use in their classrooms.   1 2 3 4 5 6

7. There is consensus on school goals among staff.   1 2 3 4 5 6

8. The staff agrees about what constitutes effective classroom instruction.   1 2 3 4 5 6

9. The leaders show concern for the staff.   1 2 3 4 5 6

10. There is a system in place to ensure high levels of success for all students.   1 2 3 4 5 6

11. The staff agrees about assessment strategies that are the most effective.   1 2 3 4 5 6

12. There are systems in place for tracking and monitoring at-risk students.   1 2 3 4 5 6

13. I know about the feedback my colleagues provide to students.   1 2 3 4 5 6

14. The leaders protect the staff from issues that detract us from focusing on learning and teaching.   1 2 3 4 5 6

15. Teachers have a voice in matters related to school improvement.   1 2 3 4 5 6

(Continued)

(Continued)

1 = Strong Disagree   2 = Disagree   3 = Somewhat Disagree
4 = Somewhat Agree   5 = Agree   6 = Strongly Agree

16. Students meet with success because of interventions that are in place.   1   2   3   4   5   6

17. I am aware of the teaching practices used by others on staff.   1   2   3   4   5   6

18. Teachers actively participate in setting school-wide improvement goals.   1   2   3   4   5   6

Scoring:

Overall Score—sum of the scores for all 18 items divided by 18.

Advanced Teacher Influence Scale

Sum of items 1, 5, and 15 _____ divided by 3 = _____

Goal Consensus Scale

Sum of items 2, 7, and 18 _____ divided by 3 = _____

Teachers' Knowledge About One Another's Work

Sum of items 6, 13, and 17 _____ divided by 3 = _____

Cohesive Staff

Sum of items 4, 8, and 11 _____ divided by 3 = _____

Responsiveness of Leadership

Sum of items 3, 9, and 14 _____ divided by 3 = _____

Effective Systems of Intervention

Sum of items 10, 12, and 16 _____ divided by 3 = _____

RESOURCE K. LEADERSHIP THEORY OF ACTION

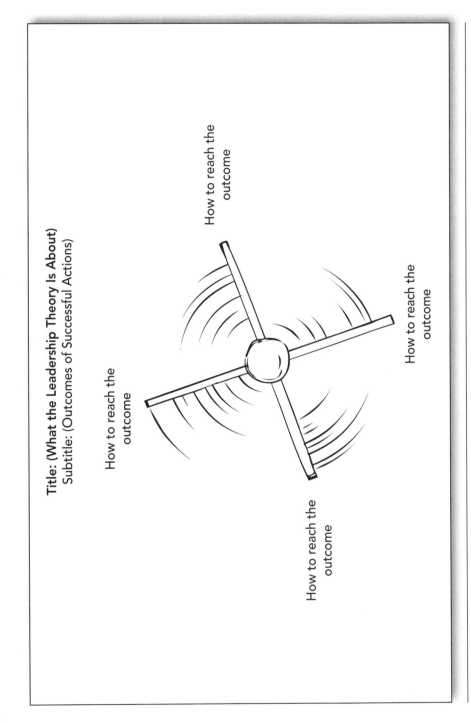

Title: (What the Leadership Theory Is About)
Subtitle: (Outcomes of Successful Actions)

How to reach the
outcome

How to reach the
outcome

How to reach the
outcome

How to reach the
outcome

Source: Adapted from Bushe, G. (2010). *Clear leadership: Sustaining real collaboration and partnership at work* (Rev. ed.). Boston, MA: Davis Black.
Propeller image courtesy of erich007/iStock/Thinkstock.

RESOURCE L. CHARACTERISTICS OF COLLABORATIVE LEADERSHIP INQUIRY CONTINUUM

Select a place along each continuum that you believe best represents your collaborative inquiry team regarding each statement.

A. Collaborative

1. Norms that enable effective collaboration are in place.

   Beginning   Developing   Applying   Innovating

2. When meeting as a learning team, our work together is owned by every member of the team.

   Beginning   Developing   Applying   Innovating

3. Decision-making authority is dispersed among individuals.

   Beginning   Developing   Applying   Innovating

4. Diversity of opinion is promoted and evident in our shared work.

   Beginning   Developing   Applying   Innovating

B. Reflective

5. Routines that encourage and enable leaders to consider and reflect on their leadership practice are in place.

   Beginning   Developing   Applying   Innovating

6. Change agents consistently use evidence to self-assess and reflect.

   Beginning   Developing   Applying   Innovating

7. Team members experiment with small moves and reflect on how well they are working.

   Beginning   Developing   Applying   Innovating

8. Actions and interactions are more intentional based on reflection.

   Beginning   Developing   Applying   Innovating

C. Learning Stance

9. Team members not only promote but also fully participate in each stage of the collaborative inquiry cycle.

   Beginning   Developing   Applying   Innovating

10. Leaders' time together is focused on teachers' learning and/or leadership practice.

    Beginning   Developing   Applying   Innovating

11. Team members are open to new ideas and actively seek new information from relevant sources to help inform next steps.

    Beginning   Developing   Applying   Innovating

12. Team members find value in the process.

    Beginning   Developing   Applying   Innovating

D. Process Is Driven by Practice

13. Our work involves examining our own and each other's practice.

    Beginning   Developing   Applying   Innovating

14. We use practice to discover strategies that work.

    Beginning   Developing   Applying   Innovating

15. We draw on outside ideas in relation to how they related to our own situation.

    Beginning   Developing   Applying   Innovating

16. Work is connected to and impacting the work of the professional learning community and wider school improvement efforts.

    Beginning   Developing   Applying   Innovating

E. Actions Informed by Evidence

17. Analysis of relevant and current data is deemed important and is an ongoing priority for the team.

    Beginning   Developing   Applying   Innovating

18. The team considers leadership actions (in light of evidence) and determines approaches that are successful and those that need to be changed.

    Beginning   Developing   Applying   Innovating

19. The team considers multiple sources of evidence to gain a well-rounded picture of their inquiry.

    Beginning   Developing   Applying   Innovating

20. Current evidence is collaboratively examined and provides a basis for considering next steps for the team's inquiry.

    Beginning   Developing   Applying   Innovating

Source: Adapted from Donohoo, J. (2013). *Collaborative inquiry for educators: A facilitator's guide to school improvement.* Thousand Oaks, CA: Corwin.

References

Adams, C., & Forsyth, P. (2006). Proximate sources of collective teacher efficacy. *Journal of Educational Administration, 44*(6), 625–642.

Allinder, R. M. (1994). The relationship between efficacy and the instructional practices of special education teachers and consultants. *Teacher Education and Special Education, 17*, 86–95.

Ashton, P. T., & Webb, R. B. (1986). *Making a difference: Teachers' sense of efficacy and student achievement*. New York, NY: Longman.

Bandura, A. (1977). Self-efficacy: Toward a unifying theory of behavioral change. *Psychological Review, 84*(2), 191–215.

Bandura, A. (1986). *Social foundations of thought and action: A social cognitive theory*. Englewood Cliffs, NJ: Prentice-Hall.

Bandura, A. (1993). Perceived self-efficacy in cognitive development and functioning. *Educational Psychologist, 28*(2), 117–148.

Bandura, A. (1997). *Self-efficacy: The exercise of control*. New York, NY: W. H. Freeman.

Beauchamp, L., Klassen, R., Parsons, J., Durksen, T., & Taylor, L. (2014). *Exploring the development of teacher efficacy through professional learning experiences*. Edmonton, Canada: Alberta Teachers' Association.

Bennett, B. (2011). Instruction: A few thinks. *Staff Development Council of Ontario Newsletter, 2*(3), 12–15.

Bonniface, L., & Henley, N. (2008). "A drop in the bucket": Collective efficacy perceptions and environmental behavior. *Australian Journal of Social Issues, 43*(3), 345–358.

Brafman, O., & Brafman, R. (2008). *Sway: The irresistible pull of irrational behavior*. New York, NY: Doubleday.

Brophy, J. E. (1983). Research on the self-fulfilling prophecy and teacher expectations. *Journal of Educational Psychology, 75*, 631–661.

Brophy, J. E., & Good, T. L. (1970). Teachers' communication of differential expectations for children's classroom performance. *Journal of Educational Psychology, 61*, 365–374.

Browning, C., Burrington, L., Leventhal, T., & Brooks-Gunn, J. (2008). Neighborhood structural inequality, collective efficacy, and sexual risk behavior among urban youth. *Journal of Health and Social Behavior, 49*, 269–285.

Bruce, C., & Flynn, T. (2013). Assessing the effects of collaborative professional learning: Efficacy shifts in a three-year mathematics study. *Alberta Journal of Educational Research, 58*(4), 691–709.

Bruce, C., & Ross, J. (2008). A model for increasing reform implementation and teacher efficacy: Teacher peer coaching in grades 3 and 6 mathematics. *Canadian Journal of Education, 31*(2), 346–370.

Bushe, G. (2010). *Clear leadership: Sustaining real collaboration and partnership at work* (Rev. ed.). Boston, MA: Davis Black.

City, E., Elmore, R., Fiarman, S., & Teitel, L. (2009). *Instructional rounds in education: A network approach to improving teaching and learning.* Cambridge, MA: Harvard Education Press.

Conroy, P. (2009). *The water is wide.* New York, NY: Random House.

Csikszentmihalyi, M. (1990). *Flow: The psychology of optimal experience.* New York, NY: HarperCollins.

Darling-Hammond, L., Wei, R., Andree, A., Richardson, N., & Orphanos, S. (2009). *Professional learning in the learning profession: A status report on teacher development in the United States and abroad.* Dallas, TX: National Staff Development Council.

Deci, E. (1995). *Why we do what we do: Understanding self-motivation.* New York, NY: Penguin.

Derrington, M., & Angelle, P. (2013). Teacher leadership and collective efficacy: Connections and links. *International Journal of Teacher Leadership, 4*(1), 1–13.

Donohoo, J. (2013). *Collaborative inquiry for educators: A facilitator's guide to school improvement.* Thousand Oaks, CA: Corwin.

Donohoo, J., & Velasco, M. (2016). *The transformative power of collaborative inquiry: Realizing change in schools and classrooms.* Thousand Oaks, CA: Corwin.

DuFour, R. (1998). Why celebrate? It sends a vivid message about what is valued. *Journal of Staff Development, 19*(4), 58–59.

DuFour, R., DuFour, R., Eaker, R., & Karhanek, G. (2010). *Raising the bar and closing the gap: Whatever it takes.* Bloomington, IN: Solution Tree Press.

Dweck, C. (2008). *Mindset: A new psychology of success.* New York, NY: Random House.

Eells, R. (2011). *Meta-analysis of the relationship between collective efficacy and student achievement* (Doctoral dissertation). Paper 133. http://ecommons.luc.edu/luc_diss/133

Elmore, R. (2008). *School reform from the inside out: Policy, practice, and performance.* Cambridge, MA: Harvard Education Press.

Escobedo, A. (2012). Teacher perceptions of the effects of school celebrations of success on collective efficacy beliefs (Doctoral dissertation). Retrieved from Gradworks (3533407)

Fichtman Dana, N., Thomas, C., & Boynton, S. (2011). *Inquiry: A districtwide approach to staff and student learning.* Thousand Oaks, CA: Corwin.

Filbin, J. (2008). *Examining the impact of changes in data-driven teaching and leading on collective efficacy.* (Doctoral dissertation). Retrieved from Gradworks (3320581)

Fletcher, A. (2003). *Meaningful student involvement: Guide to inclusive school change.* Retrieved from https://soundout.org/wp-content/uploads/2015/07/MSI_Guide_to_Inclusive_School_Change.pdf

Fullan, M., & Quinn, J. (2016). *Coherence: The right drivers in action for schools, districts, and systems.* Thousand Oaks, CA: Corwin.

Fuller, B., & Izu, J. (1986). Explaining school cohesion: What shapes the organizational beliefs of teachers? *American Journal of Education, 94*(4), 501–535.

Gallimore, R., Ermeling, B., Saunders, W., & Goldenberg, C. (2009). Moving the learning of teaching closer to practice: Teacher education implications of school-based inquiry teams. *Elementary School Journal, 109*(5), 537–553.

Georgiou, S., Christou, C., Stavrinides, P., & Panaoura, G. (2002). Teacher attributions of student failure and teacher behavior toward the failing student. *Psychology in the Schools, 39*(5), 583–595.

Gibbs, S., & Powell, B. (2012). Teacher efficacy and pupil behavior: The structure of teachers' individual and collective beliefs and their relationship with numbers of pupils excluded from school. *British Journal of Educational Psychology, 82*, 564–584.

Goddard, R. (2001). Collective efficacy: A neglected construct in the study of schools and student achievement. *Journal of Educational Psychology, 93*(3), 467–476.

Goddard, R. (2002). Collective efficacy and school organization: A multilevel analysis of teacher influence in schools. *Theory and Research in Educational Administration, 1*, 169–184.

Goddard, R., & Hoy, W. (2003). Collective efficacy scale. Retrieved from http://www.waynekhoy.com/pdfs/collective-efficacy-long.pdf

Goddard, R., Hoy, W., & Woolfolk Hoy, A. (2000). Collective teacher efficacy: Its meaning, measure, and impact on student achievement. *American Educational Research Journal, 37*(2), 479–507.

Goddard, R., Hoy, W., & Woolfolk Hoy, A. (2004). Collective efficacy beliefs: Theoretical developments, empirical evidence, and future directions. *American Educational Research Association, 33*(3), 3–13.

Goddard, R., & Skrla, L. (2006). The influence of school social composition on teachers' collective efficacy beliefs. *Educational Administration Quarterly, 42*(2), 216–235.

Graham, S. (1990). Communicating low ability in the classroom: Bad things good teachers sometimes do. In S. Graham & V. Folkes (Eds.), *Attribution theory: Applications to achievement, mental health and interpersonal conflict*. Hillsdale, NJ: Lawrence Erlbaum.

Hargreaves, A., & Fullan, M. (2012). *Professional capital: Transforming teaching in every school*. New York, NY: Teachers' College Press.

Hart, R. A. (1992). Children's participation: From tokenism to citizenship. *Innocenti Essays, 4*. Retrieved from https://www.unicef-irc.org/publications/pdf/childrens_participation.pdf

Hattie, J. (2009). *Visible learning: A synthesis of over 800 meta-analyses relating to achievement*. New York, NY: Routledge.

Hattie, J. (2012). *Visible learning for teachers: Maximizing impact on learning*. New York, NY: Routledge.

Hattie, J. (2015). *What works best in education: The politics of collaborative expertise*. London, UK: Pearson.

Hattie, J. (2016). Third Annual Visible Learning Conference (subtitled Mindframes and Maximizers), Washington, DC, July 11, 2016.

Heath, C., & Heath, D. (2010). *Switch: How to change things when change is hard.* New York, NY: Random House.

Hirsh, S., & Killion, J. (2007). *The learning educator: A new era for professional learning.* Oxford, OH: National Staff Development Council.

Horton, J., & Martin, B. (2013). The role of the district administration within professional learning communities. *International Journal of Leadership in Education, 16*(1), 55–70.

Hoy, W. K., Sweetland, S. R., & Smith, P. A. (2002). Toward an organizational model of achievement in high schools: The significance of collective efficacy. *Educational Administration Quarterly, 38*(1), 77–93.

Jeynes, W. (2007). The relationship between parental involvement and urban secondary school student academic achievement: A meta-analysis. *Urban Education, 42*(1), 82–110.

Johnson, S. (2012). *The impact of collaborative structures on perceived collective efficacy* (Doctoral dissertation). Retrieved from ERIC (ED549482)

Kanter, R. (2006). *Confidence: How winning streaks and losing streaks begin & end.* New York, NY: Random House.

Katz, S. (2015). *What are we learning about supervisory officer learning? Learning how the SO visit can build principal and vice-principal instructional leadership capacity.* Oakville, Canada: Ontario Public Supervisory Officers' Association.

Katz, S., & Dack, L. A. (2013). *Intentional interruption: Breaking down learning barriers to transform professional practice.* Thousand Oaks, CA: Corwin.

Katz, S., Earl, L., & Ben Jaafar, S. (2009). *Building and connecting learning communities: The power of networks for school improvement.* Thousand Oaks, CA: Corwin.

Kazemi, E., & Franke, M. (2004). Teacher learning in mathematics: Using student work to promote collective inquiry. *Journal of Mathematics Teacher Education, 7,* 203–235.

Klassen, R. (2010). Teacher stress: The mediating role of collective efficacy beliefs. *Journal of Educational Research, 103,* 342–350.

Knight, J. (n.d.). *Another freakin' thing we've got to do: Teacher perceptions of professional development.* Lawrence: University of Kansas Center for Research on Learning.

Knobloch, S. (2007). *Teacher participation in decision making and collective efficacy.* Dissertation. University of Virginia. (Doctoral dissertation). Retrieved from ProQuest (UMI3260669)

Kurz, T. B., & Knight, S. (2003). An exploration of the relationship among teacher efficacy, collective teacher efficacy, and goal consensus. *Learning Environments Research, 7,* 111–128.

Langer, G., & Colton, A. (2005). Looking at student work. *Education Leadership, 62*(5), 22–26.

Latham, G., & Locke, E. (2006). Enhancing the benefits and overcoming the pitfalls of goal setting. *Organizational Dynamics, 35*(4), 332–340.

Learning Forward Ontario. (2014). The power of protocols. Retrieved from http://learningforwardontario.ca/files/Power_of_Protocols.pdf

Lee, J., Zhang, Z., & Yin, H. (2011). A multilevel analysis of the impact of a professional learning community, faculty trust in colleagues and collective efficacy on teacher commitment to students. *Teaching and Teacher Education, 27,* 820–830.

Leithwood, K., & Jantzi, D. (2008). Linking leadership to student learning: The contributions of leader efficacy. *Educational Administration Quarterly, 44*(4), 496–528.

Leithwood, K., & Sun, P. (2009). Transformational school leadership effects on schools, teacher, and students. In W. Hoy & M. DiPaola (Eds.), *Studies in school improvement.* Charlotte, NC: Information Age.

Leroy, N., & Bressoux, P., Sarrazin, P., & Trouilloud, D. (2007). Impact of teachers' implicit theories and perceived pressures on the establishment of an autonomy supportive climate. *European Journal of Psychology of Education, 22*(4), 529–545.

Lewis, S. (2009). *The contribution of elements of teacher collaboration to individual and collective teacher efficacy.* (Doctoral dissertation). Retrieved from ProQuest (UMI3353824)

Little, J. W. (1990). The persistence of privacy: Autonomy and initiative in teachers' professional relations. *Teacher College Record, 91*(4), 509–536.

Liu, H., Hu, B., & Hu, X. (2015). Modeling and simulation of the collective efficacy of distributed organizations: Toward an interdependent network. *Simulation: Transactions of the Society for Modeling and Simulation International, 91*(5), 479–500.

Marzano, R. (2003). *What works in schools: Translating research into action.* Alexandria, VA: Association for Supervision and Curriculum Development.

Moolenaar, A., Sleegers, P., & Daly, A. (2012). Teaming up: Linking collaboration networks, collective efficacy, and student achievement. *Teaching and Teacher Education, 28,* 251–262.

Nelson, T., Deuel, A., Slavit, D., & Kennedy, A. (2010). Leading deep conversations in collaborative inquiry groups. *Clearing House, 83,* 175–179.

Newmann, F. M., Rutter, R. A., & Smith, M. S. (1989). Organizational factors that affect school sense of efficacy, community, and expectations. *Sociology of Education, 62,* 221–238.

Pink, D. (2009). *Drive: The surprising truth about what motivates us.* New York, NY: Penguin.

Preus, J. (2011). *Examining an inquiry-based approach for new teacher training.* (Doctoral dissertation). Retrieved from ERIC (ED533988)

Protheroe, N. (2008). Teacher efficacy: What is it and does it matter? *Principal, 87*(5), 42–45.

Ramos, M., Silva, S., Pontes, F., Fernandez, A., & Nina, K. (2014). Collective teacher efficacy beliefs: A critical review of the literature. *International Journal of Humanities and Social Science, 4*(7), 179–188.

Reeves, D. (2008). *Reframing teacher leadership to improve your school.* Alexandria, VA: Association for Supervision and Curriculum Development.

Reeves, D. (2010). *Transforming professional development into student results.* Alexandria, VA: Association for Supervision and Curriculum Development.

Reichert, F. (2015). How collective identities affect political interest and political efficacy among migrants. *Journal of Identity and Migration Studies, 9*(1), 2–98.

Research, Evaluation and Data Management Team of the Literacy and Numeracy Secretariat. (2011). *Learning in the field: The student work study teachers initiative, 2009–2010.* Toronto, Canada: Ontario Ministry of Education. Retrieved from http://www.edu.gov.on.ca/eng/literacynumeracy/research/swst.pdf

Rincon-Gallardo, S., & Fullan, M. (2016). Essential features of effective networks in education. *Journal of Professional Capital and Community, 1*(1), 5–22.

Robbins, P. (2015). *Peer coaching to enrich professional practice, school culture, and student learning.* Alexandria, VA: Association for Supervision and Curriculum Development.

Robinson, V., Hohepa, M., & Lloyd, C. (2009). *School leadership and student outcomes: Identifying what works and why.* Best evidence synthesis iteration [BES]. Auckland: New Zealand Ministry of Education.

Rosenthal, R. (1997). *Interpersonal expectancy effects: A forty year perspective.* Paper presented at the American Psychological Association Convention, Chicago, IL.

Rosenthal, R., & Babad, E. (1985). Pygmalion in the gymnasium. *Educational Leadership, 43*(1), 36–39.

Rosenthal, R., & Fode, K. (1963). The effect of experimenter bias on performance of the albino rat. *Behavioral Science, 8,* 183–189.

Rosenthal, R., & Jacobson, L. (1963). Teachers' expectancies: Determinants of pupils' IQ gains. *Psychological Reports, 19,* 115–118.

Rosenthal, R., & Jacobson, L. (1968). *Pygmalion in the classroom: Teacher expectation and pupils' intellectual development.* New York, NY: Holt, Rinehart and Winston.

Ross, J., & Bruce, C. (2007). Professional development effects on teacher efficacy: Results of randomized field trial. *Journal of Educational Research, 101*(1), 50–60.

Ross, J., & Gray, P. (2006). Transformational leadership and teacher commitment to organizational values: The mediating effects of collective teacher efficacy. *School Effectiveness and School Improvement, 17*(2), 179–199.

Ross, J., Hogaboam-Gray, A., & Gray, P. (2004). Prior student achievement, collaborative school processes, and collective teacher efficacy. *Leadership and Policy in Schools, 3*(3), 163–188.

Rubie-Davis, C., Hattie, J., Hamilton, R. (2006). Expecting the best for students: Teacher expectations and academic outcomes. *British Journal of Educational Psychology, 76*(3), 429–444.

Ryan, R., & Deci, E. (2000). Intrinsic and extrinsic motivations: Classic definitions and new directions. *Contemporary Educational Psychology, 25,* 54–67.

Schaar, J. (1989). *Legitimacy in the modern state.* New Brunswick, NJ: Transaction Publishers.

Senge, P. (1990). *The fifth discipline: The art and practice of the learning organization.* New York, NY: Doubleday.

Senge, P., Scharmer, C., Jaworski, J., & Flowers, B. (2004). *Presence: An exploration of profound change in people, organizations, and society.* New York, NY: Doubleday.

Sharratt, L., & Planche, B. (2016). *Leading collaborative learning: Empowering excellence*. Thousand Oaks, CA: Corwin.

Sorlie, M., & Torsheim, T. (2011). Multilevel analysis of the relationship between collective teacher efficacy and problem behavior in school. *School Effectiveness and School Improvement, 22*(2), 175–191.

Sousa, D. (2011). *How the brain learns* (4th ed.). Thousand Oaks, CA: Corwin.

Sousa, D. (2013). Engaging thought leaders: An interview with Dr. David Sousa. *Learning Forward Ontario Newsletter, 4*(3), 8–10.

Southern, N. (2015). Framing inquiry: The art of engaging great questions. In G. Buche & R. Marshak (Eds.), *Dialogic organization development*. Oakland, CA: Berrett-Koehler.

Sparks, D. (2007). *Leading for results: Transforming teaching, learning, and relationships in schools* (2nd ed.). Thousand Oaks, CA: Corwin.

Sunstein, C., & Hastie, R. (2015). *Wiser: Getting beyond groupthink to make groups smarter*. Boston, MA: Harvard Business School Publishing.

Tasan, A. (2000). *Teacher efficacy: Context of diversity*. (Doctoral dissertation). Paper AAI9963293 http://digitalcommons.uconn.edu/dissertations/AAI9963293

Tough, P. (2012). *How children succeed: Grit, curiosity, and the hidden power of character*. New York, NY: Houghton Mifflin Harcourt.

Tschannen-Moran, M. (n.d.). Collective teacher belief scale. Retrieved from http://wmpeople.wm.edu/asset/index/mxtsch/ctb

Tschannen-Moran, M., & Barr, M. (2004). Fostering student learning: The relationship of collective teacher efficacy and student achievement. *Leadership and Policy in Schools, 3*(3), 189–209.

Tschannen-Moran, M., & McMaster, P. (2009). Sources of self-efficacy: Four professional development formats and their relationship to self-efficacy and implementation of a new teaching strategy. *Elementary School Journal, 110*(2), 228–245.

Van Barneveld, C. (2008, August). Using data to improve student achievement. *What works? Research into practice*. Toronto, Canada: Ontario Ministry of Education and The Literacy Numeracy Secretariat.

Voelkel, Jr., R. (2011). *A case study of the relationship between collective efficacy and professional learning communities*. (Doctoral dissertation). Retrieved from Gradworks (3449371)

Wang, M. C., Haertel, G. D., & Walberg, H. J. (1993). Toward a knowledge base for school learning. *Review of Educational Research, 64*, 249–294.

Ware, H., & Kitsantas, A. (2007). Teacher and collective efficacy beliefs as predictors of professional commitment. *Journal of Educational Research, 100*(5), 303–310.

Weinstein, R. S. (2002). *Reaching higher: The power of expectations in schooling*. Cambridge, MA: Harvard University Press.

Wells, W., Schafer, J., Varano, S., & Bynum, T. (2006). Neighborhood residents' production of order: The effects of collective efficacy on responses to neighborhood problems. *Crime & Delinquency, 52*(4), 523–550.

Wheatley, M. (1992). *Leadership and the new science: Learning about organization from an orderly universe*. Oakland, CA: Berrett-Koehler.

Woolfolk, A., Rosoff, B., & Hoy, W. (1990). Teachers' sense of efficacy and their beliefs about managing students. *Teaching and Teacher Education, 6*(2), 137–148.

Zumbrunn, S., Tadlock, J., & Roberts, E. (2011). *Encouraging self-regulated learning in the classroom: A review of the literature*. Richmond: Metropolitan Educational Research Consortium, Virginia Commonwealth University.

Index

Roberts, E., 22
Robinson, V., 30, 44, 45
Rosenthal, R., 15, 16, 18, 19
Rosoff, B., 22
Ross, J., 14, 25, 29, 32, 33, 54, 68, 70
Rubie-Davis, C., 20
Ryan, R., 22

Sarrazin, P., 23
Saunders, W., 63
Schaar, J., 72, 104
Scharmer, C., 72
School Visits Protocol, 73, 106–107
Self-efficacy expectation, 3, 4, 11
Self-fulfilling prophecies, 15
    defensive pessimism and, 18–20
    Golem Effect and, 15, 17–18,
        19, 20
    Pygmalion Effect and, 15–16,
        17 (figure), 19
    See also Collective efficacy
        consequences; Expectancy
        effects
Senge, P., 72
Shared Vision Development
    Protocol, 72–73, 104–105
Sharratt, L., 56, 58
Silva, S., 4
Skrla, L., 71
Sleegers, P., 4, 59
Smith, P. A., 4
Socioeconomic status (SES), 1, 4, 5,
    6 (table), 71, 79
Sorlie, M., 23
Sousa, D., 81
Southern, N., 83, 84, 86
Sparks, D., 89
Stavrinides, P., 11

Student achievement:
    autonomy support orientation
        and, 21–23
    causal attributions and, 10–11
    collective teacher efficacy and,
        1, 3, 4, 5–6, 6 (table)
    curriculum-based factors in,
        5, 6 (table)
    difficult vs. complex tasks
        and, 81
    extrinsic vs. intrinsic rewards
        and, 22, 23
    influential factors, comparison
        of, 5–6, 6 (table)
    learner autonomy, facilitation
        of, 21–23
    motivation, competency
        beliefs/attribution and, 22
    school-based factors in, 5, 6,
        6 (table)
    socioeconomic status and, 1, 4,
        5, 6 (table), 71, 79
    student-centered classrooms
        and, 21
    student expectations and,
        4, 22
    students' self-concepts and, 20
    teaching practices and, 4–5
    Template for Documenting
        Student Learning and,
        66, 93
    See also Collective efficacy
        consequences; Collective
        teacher efficacy;
        Expectancy effects
Student Work Study Teacher
    (SWST) initiative, 68
Sun, P., 30

Sunstein, C., 37, 38
Sweetland, S. R., 4

Tadlock, J., 22
Tasan, A., 71
Taylor, L., 55, 66
Teacher efficacy. See Collaborative
    inquiry framework; Collective
    efficacy consequences;
    Collective efficacy
    development; Collective
    teacher efficacy; Professional
    learning opportunities
Team Success Analysis Protocol,
    69, 94–96
Teitel, L., 38, 58, 83
Template for Documenting
    Student Learning, 66, 93
Theory of action maps, 84,
    85 (figure), 115
Thomas, C., 69, 77, 83
Torsheim, T., 23
Tough, P., 22
Trouilloud, D., 23
Tschannen-Moran, M., 1, 8, 14, 23,
    27, 62, 67, 79

Van Barneveld, C., 71
Velasco, M., 83, 85

Ware, H., 24
Webb, R. B., 15
Wei, R., 51, 52
Wheatley, M., 55
Woolfolk Hoy, A., 3, 4, 7, 8, 11, 14,
    22, 40, 49
World Café Protocol, 80, 108–109

Zumbrunn, S., 22

A SAGE Publishing Company

Helping educators make the greatest impact

CORWIN HAS ONE MISSION: to enhance education through intentional professional learning.

We build long-term relationships with our authors, educators, clients, and associations who partner with us to develop and continuously improve the best evidence-based practices that establish and support lifelong learning.

THE PROFESSIONAL LEARNING ASSOCIATION

Learning Forward is a nonprofit, international membership association of learning educators committed to one vision in K–12 education: Excellent teaching and learning every day. To realize that vision, Learning Forward pursues its mission to build the capacity of leaders to establish and sustain highly effective professional learning. Information about membership, services, and products is available from www .learningforward.org.

ONTARIO
PRINCIPALS'
COUNCIL
Exemplary Leadership in Public Education

The Ontario Principals' Council (OPC) is a voluntary association for principals and vice-principals in Ontario's public school system. We believe that exemplary leadership results in outstanding schools and improved student achievement. To this end, we foster quality leadership through world-class professional services and supports. We are committed to **"quality leadership—our principal product."**

Solutions you want. Experts you trust.
Results you need.